CW01072714

impact
Foundation A

SERIES EDITORS
JoAnn (Jodi) Crandall
Joan Kang Shin

STUDENT'S BOOK AUTHOR
Katherine Stannett

NATIONAL GEOGRAPHIC
LEARNING

Australia · Brazil · Mexico · Singapore · United Kingdom · United States

Thank you to the educators who provided invaluable feedback during the development of *Impact*:

EXPERT PANEL

Márcia Ferreira, Academic Coordinator, CCBEU, Franca, Brazil

Jianwei Song, Vice-general Manager, Ensure International Education, Harbin, China

María Eugenia Flores, Academic Director, and **Liana Rojas-Binda**, Head of Recruitment & Training, Centro Cultural Costarricense-Norteamericano, San José, Costa Rica

Liani Setiawati, M.Pd., SMPK 1 BPK PENABUR Bandung, Bandung, Indonesia

Micaela Fernandes, Head of Research and Development Committee and Assessment Committee, Pui Ching Middle School, Macau

Héctor Sánchez Lozano, Academic Director, and **Carolina Tripodi**, Head of the Juniors Program, Proulex, Guadalajara, Mexico

Rosario Giraldez, Academic Director, Alianza Cultural, Montevideo, Uruguay

REVIEWERS

BRAZIL

Renata Cardoso, Colégio do Sol, Guara, DF

Fábio Delano Vidal Carneiro, Colégio Sete de Setembro, Fortaleza

Cristiano Carvalho, Centro Educacional Leonardo da Vinci, Vitória

Silvia Corrêa, Associação Alumni, São Paulo

Carol Espinosa, Associação Cultural Brasil Estados Unidos, Salvador

Marcia Ferreira, Centro Cultural Brasil Estados Unidos, Franca

Clara Haddad, ELT Consultant, São Paulo

Elaine Carvalho Chaves Hodgson, Colégio Militar de Brasília, Brasília

Thays Farias Galvão Ladosky, Associação Brasil América, Recife

Itana Lins, Colégio Anchieta, Salvador

Samantha Mascarenhas, Associação Cultural Brasil Estados Unidos, Salvador

Ann Marie Moreira, Pan American School of Bahia, Bahia

Rodrigo Ramirez, CEETEPS- Fatec Zona Sul, São Paulo

Paulo Torres, Vitória Municipality, Vitória

Renata Zainotte, Go Up Idiomas, Rio de Janeiro

CHINA

Zhou Chao, MaxEn Education, Beijing

Zhu Haojun, Only International Education, Shanghai

Su Jing, Beijing Chengxun International English School, Beijing

Jianjun Shen, Phoenix City International School, Guangzhou

COSTA RICA

Luis Antonio Quesada-Umaña, Centro Cultural Costarricense-Norteamericano, San José

INDONESIA

Luz S. Ismail, M.A., LIA Institute of Language and Vocational Training, Jakarta

Selestin Zainuddin, LIA Institute of Language and Vocational Training, Jakarta

Rosalia Dian Devitasari, SMP Kolese Kanisius, Jakarta

JAPAN

John Williams, Tezukayama Gakuen, Nara

MEXICO

Nefertiti González, Instituto Mexicano Madero, Puebla

Eugenia Islas, Instituto Tlalpan, Mexico City

Marta MM Seguí, Colegio Velmont A.C., Puebla

SOUTH KOREA

Min Yuol (Alvin) Cho, Global Leader English Education, Yong In

THAILAND

Panitnan Kalayanapong, Eduzone Co., Ltd., Bangkok

TURKEY

Damla Çaltuğ, İELEV, Istanbul

Basak Nalcakar Demiralp, Ankara Sinav College, Ankara

Humeyra Olcayli, İstanbul Bilim College, Istanbul

VIETNAM

Chantal Kruger, ILA Vietnam, Hô Chí Minh

Ai Nguyen Huynh, Vietnam USA Society, Hô Chí Minh

2

impact
Foundation A

Scope and Sequence		4
Meet the Explorers		5

STUDENT'S BOOK:

Unit 0	Welcome!	8
Unit 1	Family Matters	26
Unit 2	A Different Education	42
	Express Yourself: Text messages	58
Unit 3	Robots and Us	60
Unit 4	Part of Nature	76
	Express Yourself: Advertisement	92
	Pronunciation	162
	Irregular Verbs	166
	Social and Academic Language	167
	Cutouts	171

WORKBOOK:

Unit 0	Welcome!	2
Unit 1	Family Matters	16
Unit 2	A Different Education	26
	Units 1–2 Review	36
Unit 3	Robots and Us	38
Unit 4	Part of Nature	48
	Units 3–4 Review	58
	You Decide Activities	104

1
Family Matters
page 26

2
A Different Education
page 42

3
Robots and Us
page 60

4
Part of Nature
page 76

	1 Family Matters	2 A Different Education	3 Robots and Us	4 Part of Nature
THEME	Family and traditions	Schools around the world	People interacting with technology	People and animals and their place in nature
VOCABULARY STRATEGY	Adjective + dependent preposition	Antonyms	The *-able* ending	Compound words
SPEAKING STRATEGY	Asking and answering personal questions	Talking about likes and dislikes	Reacting	Checking facts
GRAMMAR	**Be and have got:** *I'm friendly, but my sister isn't.* **Countable and uncountable nouns:** *Are there any biscuits in the cupboard? Yes, there are. Is there any water in the bottle? Yes, there is.*	**Present simple:** Talking about routines, habits and permanent states *She doesn't have lunch at school. She goes home for lunch.* **Adverbs of frequency:** Saying how often you do something *I rarely forget to do my homework.*	**Can and can't:** Talking about ability *My robot can talk, but it can't open doors.* **Should and shouldn't:** Giving advice *They should study for this maths test. You shouldn't buy this robot. It's very expensive.*	**Quantifiers:** Talking and asking about quantity *How many different kinds of camels are there? There are two kinds of camels.* **Adverbs:** Saying how you do something *Elephants can swim very well. The three-toed sloth moves very slowly.*
READING	*Breakfast in Four Countries*	*Growth Mindset*	*Girls Can Code*	*A Wild Animal Isn't a Pet*
READING STRATEGY	Make predictions based on visuals	Identify the main idea	Identify the main point of a paragraph	Identify sequence of events
VIDEO	*Celebrating the Dead*	*Education Around the World*	*Squishy Robot Fingers*	*Into the Real Wild: Photographing Pandas with Ami Vitale*
MISSION	**Discover Your Values** National Geographic Explorer: **Max Lowe**, Photographer/Writer	**Believe in Yourself** National Geographic Explorers: **Dave and Amy Freeman**, Adventurers/Educators	**Change the World** National Geographic Explorer: **Chad Jenkins**, Computer Scientist/Roboticist	**Use Your Skills** National Geographic Explorer: **Juliana Machado Ferreira**, Conservation Biologist
WRITING	Genre: **Personal description** Focus: Connect and contrast	Genre: **Sequencing paragraph** Focus: Use sequencing words	Genre: **Contrast paragraph** Focus: Use contrast words	Genre: **Fact sheet** Focus: Categorise and label information
PRONUNCIATION	Syllables and stress	The third person *-s* and *-es* endings	The *th* sound	Short vowel sounds
EXPRESS YOURSELF	Creative Expression: **Text messages** *World Food Day* Making connections: Family, food and school		Creative Expression: **Advertisement** *Robotosaurus Rex* Making connections: Robots and animals	

Unit 1

MAX LOWE Photographer/Writer

A sense of adventure runs in Max Lowe's family. Max's father, Alex, died in a climbing accident when Max was young. Max's father inspired him. Now, Max travels with his step-father, Conrad, who is also a climber. Max writes about their adventures and takes photos to remember their experiences together.

Unit 2

DAVE AND AMY FREEMAN Adventurers/Educators

Dave and Amy Freeman were named National Geographic Adventurers of the Year in 2014. They are husband and wife. They explore by foot, kayak, canoe and even dogsled! The Freemans also record their adventures for thousands of students to watch all over the world. Their video lessons inspire students to explore.

Unit 3

CHAD JENKINS Computer Scientist/Roboticist

Chad Jenkins builds robots. He teaches his robots to do things, but he doesn't do it alone. He asks people to visit his online lab. People give Chad ideas for new things they would like to see his robots do. Chad's robots can help out around the house, or even play sports! What do you want to ask Chad's robots to do?

Unit 4

JULIANA MACHADO FERREIRA Conservation Biologist

Juliana Machado Ferreira lives in Brazil, where some people take birds from their homes in the wild to sell them as pets. When she was a child, Juliana's parents taught her to love animals. Now, Juliana teaches others to love animals and to understand their role in nature. She also uses DNA information to return birds to their homes in the wild.

Welcome!

The Alphabet

1 Listen, point and repeat. 🎧 002

Aa Bb Cc Dd Ee Ff Gg Hh Ii
Jj Kk Ll Mm Nn Oo Pp Qq Rr
Ss Tt Uu Vv Ww Xx Yy Zz

'A is for Athens.'

World map, Lisbon, Portugal

1 **Listen and repeat.** 🎧 003

Greetings and Introductions		Questions
Hi!	Hello!	What's your name?
I'm Benjamina.	My name's Tarek.	Where are you from?
This is Julia.	Good / Nice to meet you.	

2 **Read and listen.** Underline the greetings and introductions. Circle the questions in blue. 🎧 004

Nadia: Hi! I'm Nadia. What's your name?

Chang: Hi, Nadia. My name's Chang. I'm from China.

Nadia: Good to meet you, Chang.

Chang: Where are you from?

Nadia: I'm from Turkey. This is my friend Gabriel. He's from Argentina.

Chang: Hello, Gabriel. Nice to meet you.

Gabriel: Hi! Nice to meet you, too!

Mrs Martin: OK! I think we're all ready to start. Welcome to your new English class! My name is Mrs Martin. I'm from Australia.

3 **Complete the sentences with the words from the box.**

Argentinian	Chinese	Australian	Turkish

1. Nadia is _____ .

2. Chang is _____ .

3. Gabriel is _____ .

4. Mrs. Martin is _____ .

4 Listen and repeat. 🎧 005

GRAMMAR

Subject pronouns and *be*

Full forms	Contractions		Full forms	Contractions
I am	I'm		I am not	I'm not
You are	You're		You are not	You aren't
He/She/It is	He's/She's/It's		He/She/It is not	He/She/It isn't
We are	We're		We are not	We aren't
You are	You're		You are not	You aren't
They are	They're		They are not	They aren't

My name's Sara. I'm from Spain.
His name's Alan. He's from France. He isn't from Spain.

5 Look at Activity 2 again. (Circle) all the examples of the verb *be* in red.

6 Listen and match. Then make sentences. 🎧 006

Brazil	Spain	Malaysia	Bulgaria	Mexico

Bulgarian	Spanish	Mexican	Brazilian	Malaysian

1. Nor _is Malaysian. She's from Malaysia._
2. Karina _____
3. Daniel _____
4. Andrei _____
5. Alicia and Sandra _____

7 Work in groups. Imagine you are in Australia for a month to study English. Copy and complete the card to the right. Ask and answer.

Hi, I'm Junko. What's your name?

Hi, Junko. My name's Mayumi.

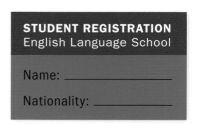

STUDENT REGISTRATION
English Language School

Name: _____

Nationality: _____

Classroom Language

1 Listen and repeat. 🎧007

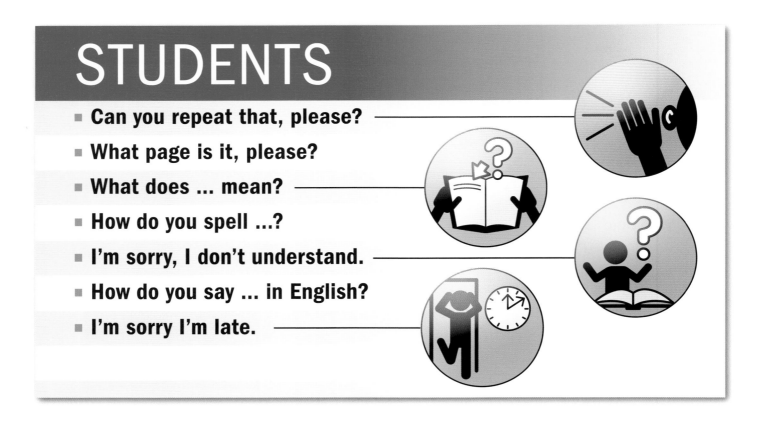

TEACHER

- Sit down, please!
- Be quiet, please!
- Open your books at page 5.
- Listen to the recording.
- Work in pairs.
- Hurry up, please!
- Close the door, please.
- Write your answers in your books.

STUDENTS

- Can you repeat that, please?
- What page is it, please?
- What does ... mean?
- How do you spell ...?
- I'm sorry, I don't understand.
- How do you say ... in English?
- I'm sorry I'm late.

2 **Read and listen.** 🎧 008

Mrs Martin:	Be quiet, please! Open your books at page 40.
Daniel:	Can you repeat that, please?
Mrs Martin:	Open your books at page 40. Let's look at the photo. He's a National Geographic Explorer. What's his name?
Nadia:	His name is Max Lowe.
Mrs Martin:	Yes, that's right. Well done, Nadia. Now let's watch ...
Alberto:	I'm sorry I'm late, Mrs Martin.
Mrs Martin:	Hurry up, please, Alberto! Gabriel, don't talk to Chang.
Gabriel:	Sorry, Mrs Martin.
Mrs Martin:	Now, let's watch ...
Alicia:	Mrs Martin, I can't see.
Mrs Martin:	Oh. Well, move your chair over here. Good. Now. Is everyone ready? Let's watch the video.

3 **Work in small groups.** Act out the conversation from Activity 2.

4 **Now make up your own conversation.** Use classroom language from Activity 1.

Months of the Year and Days of the Week

1 **Listen and repeat.** 🎧 009

January	February	March	April
May	June	July	August
September	October	November	December

2 **Listen and repeat.** 🎧 010

Monday	Tuesday	Wednesday	Thursday	Friday	Saturday	Sunday

3 **Work in pairs.** Ask and answer questions.

What day is it today?

It's Monday.

What month is it?

It's August.

Seasons

1 **Listen and repeat.** 🎧 011

spring

summer

wet season

autumn

winter

dry season

2 **Work in pairs.** Ask and answer questions.

What season is it?

It's summer.

What season is it?

It's the dry season.

Numbers

1 **Listen and repeat.** 🎧 012

1	one	first
2	two	second
3	three	third
4	four	fourth
5	five	fifth
6	six	sixth
7	seven	seventh
8	eight	eighth
9	nine	ninth
10	ten	tenth
11	eleven	eleventh
12	twelve	twelfth
13	thirteen	thirteenth
14	fourteen	fourteenth
15	fifteen	fifteenth
16	sixteen	sixteenth
17	seventeen	seventeenth

18	eighteen	eighteenth
19	nineteen	nineteenth
20	twenty	twentieth
21	twenty-one	twenty-first
22	twenty-two	twenty-second
30	thirty	thirtieth
40	forty	fortieth
50	fifty	fiftieth
60	sixty	sixtieth
70	seventy	seventieth
80	eighty	eightieth
90	ninety	ninetieth
100	one hundred	hundredth
101	one hundred and one	
235	two hundred and thirty-five	
999	nine hundred and ninety-nine	
1000	one thousand	

2 **Work in groups.** Ask and answer questions.

When's your birthday?

My birthday is on the 29th of August.

How old are you?

I'm fourteen years old.

Colours

1 Listen and repeat. 🎧 013

2 Point and say.

pink

yellow

white

brown

grey

orange

purple

red

blue

green

black

Telling the Time

1 **Listen and repeat.** 🎧 **014**

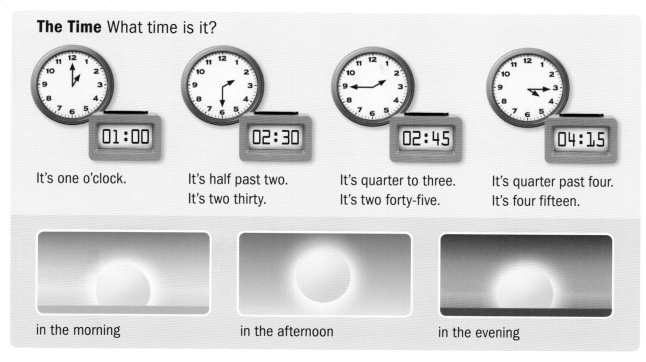

The Time What time is it?

01:00 It's one o'clock.

02:30 It's half past two.
It's two thirty.

02:45 It's quarter to three.
It's two forty-five.

04:15 It's quarter past four.
It's four fifteen.

in the morning

in the afternoon

in the evening

2 **Work in pairs.** Look at the map of Australia. Write the times in words. Then read.

Darwin
Cairns
4.30 p.m. (+1.5 hr)
5 p.m. (+2.0 hr)
3 p.m.
5.30 p.m. (+2.5 hr)
Perth
6 p.m. (+3.0 hr)
Sydney
Adelaide

What time is it in Perth?

It's _three o'clock in the afternoon_ .

What time is it in Darwin?

It's _____ .

What time is it in Cairns?

It's _____ .

What time is it in Sydney?

It's _____ .

What time is it in Adelaide?

It's _____ .

3 **Work in pairs.** Ask and answer.

Lunch is at one o'clock.

What time is ...

- lunch?
- breakfast?
- your favourite club?
- your first lesson at school
- your favourite TV programme?
- your last lesson at school?

1 **Listen and repeat.** 🎧 **015**

GRAMMAR

Object pronouns

It's for **me**.   I don't like **it**.
This is for **you**.   Come with **us**.
It belongs to **him**.   It belongs to **you**.
I'm with **her**.   It's for **them**.

2 **Listen and read.** (Circle) the object pronouns. 🎧 **016**

1. Maria: Hi, Francesco.
                     Where's Teresa?
    Francesco: I don't know.
                     She isn't at school today.
    Maria: Oh, I usually have lunch with her.

2. Stefano: I like your bike. It's really cool!
    Anna: Thank you! I love it.

3. Roberto: Who's that boy?
    Claudia: I don't know him. He's a new student here.

4. Antonio: Hurry up, Luca! It's half past three. We're late!
    Luca: I know! Mrs Martin is angry with us again!

3 (Circle) **the correct words.**

1. Who is this girl? *I / Me* don't know *she / her* .
2. *He / Him* is a very good student.
3. Where is my book? *I / Us* can't find *him / it* .
4. *Us / We* are in classroom B today.
5. *He / Him* doesn't like *we / us* .
6. Look at the shoes! I like *they / them* .

1 **Listen and repeat.** 🎧 017

GRAMMAR

Possessive adjectives

It's **my** cat. This is **its** food.
Is this **your** house? Are these **your** books?
No, it's **his** house. Yes, they're **our** books.
It's **her** bag. Where are **their** books?

2 (Circle) **the correct word.**

1. Carla's got a twin brother. *His / Her* name is Pedro.

2. They've got one cat. *Its / Their* name is Cosmo.

3. Carla and Pedro like purple. It's *his / their* favourite colour.

4. I love purple, too. It's *my / her* favourite colour!

3 **Look at the photo.** Complete the sentences with the names. (Circle) the correct word.

1. _____ likes hiking with *her / their* dad.

2. _____ 's top is blue. *His / Her* rucksack is red and black.

3. _____ 's shorts are grey. *His / Our* rucksack is green.

4. _____ 's hair is grey. _____ 's hair is a different colour. *Her / Our* hair is brown.

5. _____ and _____ like the flowers in the mountains. *Their / Its* favourite flowers are yellow.

Amy

Bai

1 Listen and repeat. 🎧 018

GRAMMAR

Possessive pronouns

This is my book. This book is **mine**.
This is your phone. This phone is **yours**.
This is his bike. This bike is **his**.
This is her bag. This bag is **hers**.
This is your house. This house is **yours**.

This is our school. This school is **ours**.
These are their shoes. These shoes are **theirs**.

Question word: Whose?
Whose house is this?
It's **mine**.

2 Listen and read. (Circle) the correct word. Then listen and check. 🎧 019

Penny: Is this your book, Ana?

Ana: No, it isn't *my / mine*. Is it *your / yours*?

Penny: No, it isn't. There's Sara! Maybe it's *her / hers*.
Sara, is this book *your / yours*?

Sara: Yes, it is. It's *my / mine*!
Thank you!

3 Complete the conversation with the words from the box.

your	yours	my	mine

Mrs Martin: Adam, where is _____ book?

Adam: I'm sorry, Mrs Martin. It isn't in _____ bag. I don't know where it is.

Mrs Martin: Jan, there are two books on your desk. Are they _____ ?

Jan: Yes, they are _____ , Mrs Martin. This is _____ English book, and this is _____ maths book.

4 Write.

her	hers	mine	yours	whose

Khaled: _____ kite is this? Is it _____ , Zain?

Zain: It isn't _____ . Is it _____ ?

Khaled: Yes. Look, _____ name is on it.

Plurals

1 **Listen and repeat.** 🎧020

singular	plural	singular	plural	singular	plural
girl	girl**s**	bus	bus**es**	child	children
boy	boy**s**	watch	watch**es**	woman	women
teacher	teacher**s**	box	box**es**	man	men
		quiz	quiz**zes**	person	people
		potato	potato**es**	mouse	mice
singular	**plural**	class	class**es**	deer	deer
baby	bab**ies**			sheep	sheep
country	countr**ies**			tooth	teeth
				foot	feet

2 **Work in pairs.** Take turns. Use a coin to move. (Heads = 1 space; tails = 2 spaces) Is the word plural? Say the singular. Is the word singular? Say the plural.

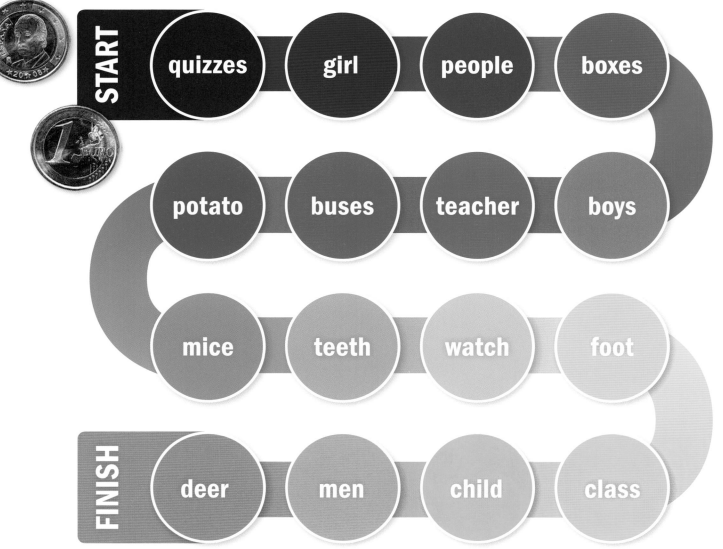

1 **Listen and repeat.** 🎧 **021**

> ### GRAMMAR
>
> **Definite and indefinite articles**
>
> There is **a** book in my bag. **The** book is red.
> There is **an** apple on the table. **The** apple is green.
> Who are **the** students in your classroom?

2 **Complete the sentences with *a*, *an* or *the*.**

1. Alberto is _____ student at my school.

2. There's _____ umbrella in my bag.

3. _____ books on this desk are mine.

4. I've got _____ new bike. _____ bike is purple.

5. A: Where is _____ English teacher?

   B: He's in _____ school office.

1 **Listen and repeat.** 🎧 **022**

> **GRAMMAR**
>
> **Demonstrative adjectives**
>
>
> **This** flower is pink.
>
>
> She wants **that** flower.
>
>
> **These** flowers are pretty.
>
>
> I like **those** orange flowers.

2 **Read the sentences.** Are the underlined words singular or plural, near or far? Tick two boxes for each sentence.

	Singular	Plural	Near	Far
1. <u>This</u> bike is red.	✓	☐	✓	☐
2. Is <u>that</u> your house?	☐	☐	☐	☐
3. <u>These</u> umbrellas are purple.	☐	☐	☐	☐
4. <u>That</u> cat is black.	☐	☐	☐	☐
5. Are <u>those</u> shoes new?	☐	☐	☐	☐
6. She wants to read <u>this</u> book.	☐	☐	☐	☐
7. Who is <u>that</u> girl?	☐	☐	☐	☐
8. <u>That</u> phone is cool!	☐	☐	☐	☐

3 **Work in pairs.** Describe things in the classroom. Use *this*, *that*, *these* and *those* to talk about them.

> This bag is big.

> Those pencils are yellow.

1 **Listen and repeat.** Where is the cat? 🎧 **023**

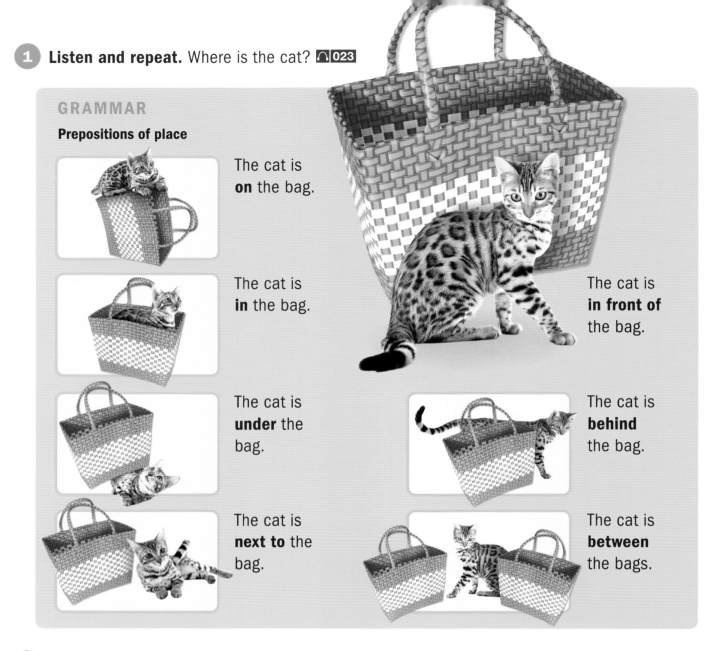

GRAMMAR

Prepositions of place

The cat is **on** the bag.

The cat is **in** the bag.

The cat is **in front of** the bag.

The cat is **under** the bag.

The cat is **behind** the bag.

The cat is **next to** the bag.

The cat is **between** the bags.

2 **Work in pairs.** Look at the pictures in Activity 1.

- Choose a picture.
- Describe where the cat is.
- Can your partner point to the correct picture?

3 **Draw a simple picture.** Don't show it to your partner. Include these things.

a table	a chair	an animal	a box
a hat	some books	some pencils	a banana

- Describe your picture to your partner.
- Use prepositions of place.
- Can your partner draw your picture?

There's a chair next to a table.
There are some books under the chair.
There's a box on the chair.

1 Listen and repeat. 🎧024

> **GRAMMAR**
>
> **Countable and uncountable nouns**
>
> | **Countable nouns** | **Uncountable nouns** |
> | --- | --- |
> | There's **an apple** on the table. | There's **some juice** on the table. |
> | There are **some apples** in the fridge. | There's **some bread** on the table. |

2 Complete the sentences with *a*, *an* or *some*.

1. There is _____*some*_____ juice and _____ bread.

2. There is _____ egg.

3. There are _____ tomatoes and _____ strawberries.

4. There is _____ cheese.

3 Talk about the food in your fridge at home.

There is some butter.

There are some tomatoes.

Family Matters

Explorers Max Lowe and Conrad Anker

'My dad was superhuman to me.'
Max Lowe

TO START

1. Look at the photo. Guess. How are the people related?

2. What does 'superhuman' mean to you?

3. Who are your heroes? Are they famous people, friends or people in your family?

1 **Do you know any famous families?**
Discuss. Then listen and read. 🎧 **025**

The Cousteau Family

Jacques Cousteau was a great marine explorer. Many people enjoy his books and films about the sea. His **son**, Philippe Sr, also loved the sea and made films about it. Now his **grandson**, Philippe Jr, and his **granddaughter**, Alexandra, want to protect the sea. 'My father and grandfather were an inspiration,' says Alexandra.

Meave and Louise Leakey working together, Kenya

The Lowe-Anker Family

Conrad Anker **is married to** Jennifer Lowe-Anker. Jennifer's first **husband**, Alex Lowe, was a very famous climber. He **died** in a climbing accident in 1999. Alex and Conrad were very close friends and Conrad is also very good at climbing. In fact, he's also a professional climber. When Alex died, Conrad helped to **take care of** Jennifer's **children**, Max, Isaac and Sam. Max now works with his **step-father**. 'Conrad is my hero and my mentor,' he says.

The Leakey Family

Palaeoanthropologists are scientists who are interested in fossils and early human life. There are three **generations** of palaeoanthropologists in the Leakey family. Mary and Louis Leakey were very famous for their important work in the 1940s and 50s. Their son, Richard Leakey, is also interested in early human life. Richard and his **wife**, Meave, have got two **daughters**, Louise and Samira. Meave and Louise now work together.

2 **LEARN NEW WORDS Listen and repeat.** 🎧 026

3 **Work in pairs.** Name one of your heroes. What do you know about his or her family? Take notes. Compare your notes with your partner's.

4 **Read and write the words from the list.**

| child | daughter | died | husband | is married to | son | step-father | wife |

　　　Max Lowe is a National Geographic photographer and writer. He travels around the world and takes photos of amazing places. He is the _____ of Jennifer Lowe-Anker and Alex Lowe. Alex was Jennifer's first _____ . He _____ in a climbing accident in 1999, when Max was a young _____ . Now, Jennifer _____ another famous climber, Conrad Anker. Conrad is Max's _____ . Max and Conrad enjoy climbing and travelling together.

5 **LEARN NEW WORDS Listen to these words and match them to their definitions. Then listen and repeat.** 🎧 **027 028**

| enjoy | famous | good at | interested in |

_____　1. able to do something well

_____　2. known by many people

_____　3. wanting to know more about something

_____　4. like doing something

6 **YOU DECIDE Choose an activity.**

1. **Work independently.** Interview one of your classmates. Find out about the different people in your classmate's family. Make a list of what your classmate is good at, and what he or she is interested in.

2. **Work in pairs.** Imagine your family is famous. Tell your partner about the different people in your family. What are they famous for?

3. **Work in groups.** Choose one of the families from this section. Draw and illustrate their family tree.

Max Lowe

SPEAKING STRATEGY 🎧029

Asking and answering personal questions

What's your brother's **name**? His name's Lucas.
What's your favourite sport? **My favourite** sport **is** football.
Where do you live? **I live in** Recife.
Where are your grandparents **from**? **They're from** Kyoto.

1 **Listen.** How do these speakers ask and answer questions? Write the phrases you hear. 🎧030

2 **Read and complete the dialogue.**

Gina: Is this a photo of your family?

Marco: Yes, it is.

Gina: It's a great photo.

　　　　_____ baby sister's name?

Marco: _____ Gabriela.

Gina: And _____ your mum from?

Marco: _____ Rosario.

Gina: _____ ?

Marco: We live in Buenos Aires.

Gina: _____ place in Argentina?

Marco: My favourite place is Mendoza. My grandparents live there. It's really beautiful.

3 **Work in pairs.** Take turns throwing the cube. Ask and answer questions.

what / favourite / film
what / mum's / name
where / dad / from

Go to page 171.

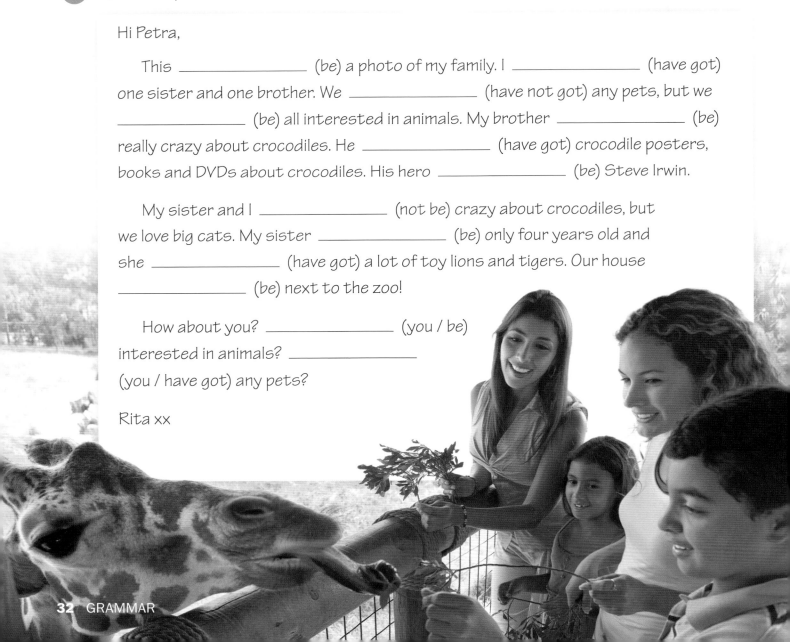

Be

I'm friendly, but my sister **isn't**.

My grandparents **are** interested in photography.

Is your mum good at sport?

Have got

I**'ve got** two brothers.

My aunt **hasn't got** any children.

Have you got any brothers or sisters?

1 **Listen.** You will hear six sentences about Joel's family. Circle the correct form of the verbs you hear. 032

1. hasn't got   haven't got
2. 'm   's
3. is   are

4. 's   are
5. 's got   've got
6. isn't   aren't

2 **Read.** Complete the sentences with the correct form of the verbs in brackets.

Hi Petra,

    This _____ (be) a photo of my family. I _____ (have got) one sister and one brother. We _____ (have not got) any pets, but we _____ (be) all interested in animals. My brother _____ (be) really crazy about crocodiles. He _____ (have got) crocodile posters, books and DVDs about crocodiles. His hero _____ (be) Steve Irwin.

    My sister and I _____ (not be) crazy about crocodiles, but we love big cats. My sister _____ (be) only four years old and she _____ (have got) a lot of toy lions and tigers. Our house _____ (be) next to the zoo!

    How about you? _____ (you / be) interested in animals? _____ (you / have got) any pets?

Rita xx

LEARN NEW WORDS Listen to learn about Clare's brothers. Then listen and repeat. 🎧 033 034

My brothers, Charlie and Peter, are very **friendly**.

Charlie is **messy** and **noisy**.

Sometimes Peter is a bit **mean** to Charlie. He thinks Charlie is **annoying**. But Charlie is really **funny**.

4 **Work in pairs.** Describe your family. Who is messy? Who is friendly? Is anyone a bit mean sometimes?

5 **Play a game in groups.**

1. Work together to make a list of families from your favourite books, films and TV programmes.

2. Work independently. Write a sentence about each character. Begin 'This person is ...' and use at least one word from the box below.

annoying	friendly	funny	good (at)
interested (in)	mean	messy	noisy

This person is very good at singing.

This person is really funny.

3. Read each other's sentences and try to guess the characters.

1 **BEFORE YOU READ Discuss in pairs.**
Look at the title and the photo. What do you think the reading is about?

2 **LEARN NEW WORDS Find these words in the reading.** Which word is a more general word? Then listen and repeat. 🎧 035

> **breakfast**   **dinner**   **lunch**   **meal**

3 **WHILE YOU READ Underline the numbers in the text.** 🎧 036

A special Saturday morning breakfast in Turkey

BREAKFAST

DIFFERENT WAYS TO START THE DAY AROUND THE WORLD

What food does your family eat in the morning? What is your favourite breakfast food? Is your meal at breakfast very different from your meal at lunch or dinner? Do you eat the same things as your friends?

Different families around the world have got very different diets. Do you know what people have for breakfast in other parts of the world?

In Malawi, Emily, aged seven, starts the day at six in the morning. She lives with her grandmother and seven other family members. Her breakfast is porridge made from flour. She also has vegetables and drinks tea.

Oyku is nine years old. She's from Turkey. She has brown bread with olives, jam, tomatoes, eggs and a lot of different types of cheese.

Nathanaël is six and he lives in France. From Monday to Friday, Nathanaël has fruit, cereal and bread with his grandmother's homemade jam for breakfast. At the weekends he eats croissants. His favourite food, though, is pancakes (or 'crêpes' in French) with hot chocolate. In France, children drink hot chocolate from a bowl.

Viv, from the Netherlands, is five years old. She has bread with sweet sprinkles on top. This is a very popular breakfast in the Netherlands. The Dutch eat 750,000 slices of bread with chocolate sprinkles every day!

IN FOUR COUNTRIES

4 AFTER YOU READ **Answer the questions.**

1. Who eats a special food at the weekend?
2. Who lives with her grandmother?
3. Who is from the Netherlands?
4. In which country do children drink from a bowl?
5. Where is Oyku from?

5 **Work in pairs.** Find numbers in the text to complete these sentences.

1. There are _____ people in Emily's family.
2. Every day, people in the Netherlands eat _____ slices of bread with chocolate sprinkles.
3. Nathanaël is _____ years old.
4. Emily gets up at _____ in the morning.

6 **Discuss in groups.**

1. Look at the food in the photo. Do you eat similar food? Do you want to try some of the food in the photo? Which food?
2. What do you think we can learn from the text?
3. What differences do you notice between the people in the text?

1 BEFORE YOU WATCH **Discuss in pairs.** Which festivals and holidays do you celebrate together with your family? How do you celebrate them?

2 **Work in pairs.** You're going to watch *Celebrating the Dead*. Look at the photo. Why do you think the girls are smiling? Discuss your ideas.

3 WHILE YOU WATCH **Circle the things you see.** Watch scene 1.1.

party hats	a book
a guitar	food
flowers	balloons

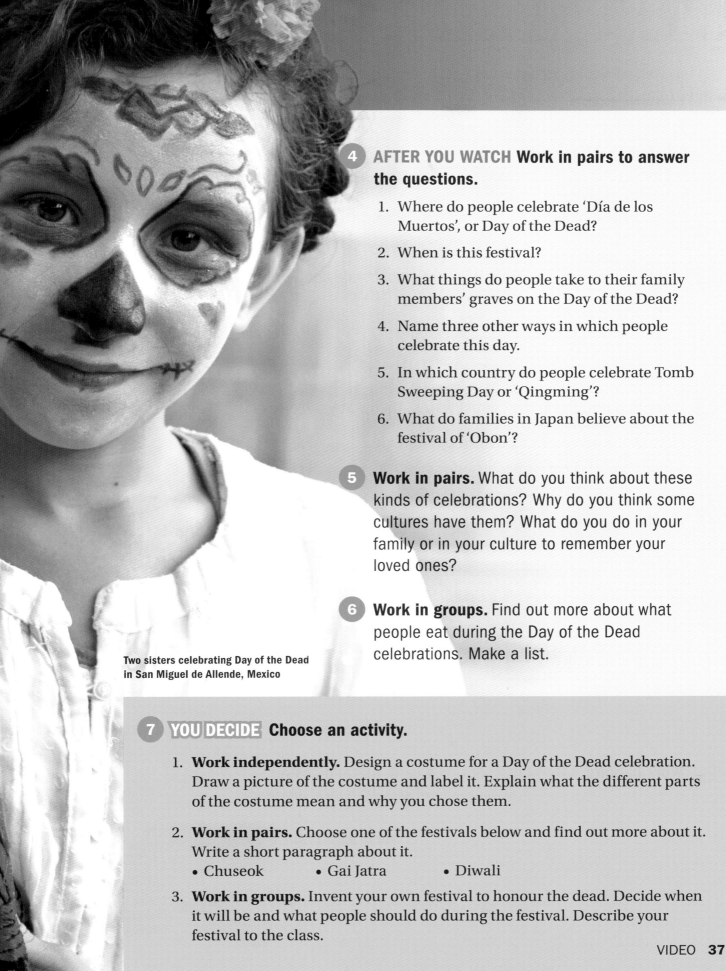

4 **AFTER YOU WATCH** **Work in pairs to answer the questions.**

1. Where do people celebrate 'Día de los Muertos', or Day of the Dead?

2. When is this festival?

3. What things do people take to their family members' graves on the Day of the Dead?

4. Name three other ways in which people celebrate this day.

5. In which country do people celebrate Tomb Sweeping Day or 'Qingming'?

6. What do families in Japan believe about the festival of 'Obon'?

5 **Work in pairs.** What do you think about these kinds of celebrations? Why do you think some cultures have them? What do you do in your family or in your culture to remember your loved ones?

6 **Work in groups.** Find out more about what people eat during the Day of the Dead celebrations. Make a list.

Two sisters celebrating Day of the Dead in San Miguel de Allende, Mexico

7 **YOU DECIDE** **Choose an activity.**

1. **Work independently.** Design a costume for a Day of the Dead celebration. Draw a picture of the costume and label it. Explain what the different parts of the costume mean and why you chose them.

2. **Work in pairs.** Choose one of the festivals below and find out more about it. Write a short paragraph about it.
   • Chuseok   • Gai Jatra   • Diwali

3. **Work in groups.** Invent your own festival to honour the dead. Decide when it will be and what people should do during the festival. Describe your festival to the class.

Countable and uncountable nouns

Countable nouns	Uncountable nouns
Are there any biscuits in the cupboard?	**Is there any** water in the bottle?
Yes, there are. **There are some** chocolate biscuits, but **there aren't any** ginger biscuits.	Yes, there is. And **there's some** juice in the fridge.
Is there a banana in your bag?	**Is there any** bread at the shop?
No, there isn't. But **there is an** apple.	No, there isn't. **There isn't any** bread, but **there's some** rice.

1 **Listen to the conversation.** Write *C* for countable and *U* for uncountable next to each word. 🎧038

_____ kebab	_____ beefburger	_____ lettuce	_____ tomato
_____ juice	_____ water	_____ banana	_____ honey

2 **Work in pairs.** Circle the correct words. Then write *some* or *any*.

Today is my sister's tenth birthday and my whole family is here for her birthday meal. There *is /* (*are*) ____some____ cheese sandwiches and there *is / are* _____ crisps. There *isn't / aren't* _____ sweets because my sister doesn't like sweets, but there *is / are* _____ biscuits and there *is / are* a big chocolate cake. There *is / are* also _____ fruit – there *is / are* _____ grapes and there *is / are* _____ strawberries. There *isn't / aren't* _____ juice, but there *is / are* _____ coffee in a large pot and there *is / are* _____ water.

3 **Work in pairs.** Take turns choosing a card. Ask and answer questions using the words on the card with *Is there / Are there*.

Is there any water in the bottle?

Yes, there is.

Go to page 173.

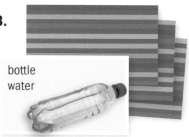

bottle
water

WRITING

We use joining words, such as *and* and *but*, to connect information in a sentence. We use *and* to connect two similar pieces of information.

> She's got long hair **and** blue eyes.

We use *but* to contrast two different pieces of information.

> My brother is very friendly, **but** my sister is quite mean.

1 **Read the model.** How does the writer connect and contrast information? Underline the sentences with *and* and *but*.

My Grandfather

I've got one grandfather – my grandfather Miguel. Grandfather Miguel is from Mexico, but now he lives with us in Spain. He's 72 years old, but he's very fit and active. He's got short grey hair and brown eyes. He's quite tall and he's got a very loud voice. He's really funny and friendly. All my friends like him. His favourite meal is breakfast, and he loves the Mexican dish 'huevos rancheros' – eggs with tomatoes and chilli. He's very interested in music and he's got three guitars. He enjoys playing them, but he isn't very good at it!

2 **Work in pairs.** What information does the writer include about his grandfather? Tick the information that is in the paragraph.

_____ his name   _____ his personality   _____ his favourite animals

_____ his appearance   _____ his friends   _____ his interests

3 **Write.** Describe a member of your family. Remember to use *and* and *but* to connect and contrast information.

Discover Your Values

'The things you value in life stem from the very beginning.'

Max Lowe

National Geographic Explorer, Photographer and Writer

1. Watch scene 1.2.

2. Max Lowe is from a family of climbers. He is a photographer and writer. Max travels around the world and takes photos of beautiful places. How is his career connected to his family?

3. What things are important to your family? Are they important to you? How?

Make an Impact

1 **Draw a family tree.**

· Find out about four generations of a family.

· Draw a family tree to show how they are all in the same family.

· Write sentences about the people in the family tree. Describe the different relationships.

2 **Make a poster about your family's breakfast.**

· Keep a record of everything your family eats for breakfast.

· Design a poster with pictures and facts about the food.

· Display your poster in the classroom. Answer your classmates' questions about the information on the poster.

3 **Make a class family album.**

· Bring in some of your favourite family photos.

· Write a few sentences about each photo.

· Stick the photos and sentences in a book to create a class family album.

A Different Education

'It's a big world. We still have
a lot to learn and share.'
Amy Freeman

Children in a boat
classroom, Bangladesh

TO START

1. Look at the photo. What is unusual about this school?

2. Do you want to visit this school? Explain why or why not.

3. Imagine your perfect classroom. Where is it? Is it outside or inside? What does it look like? How many students are there?

1 **What do you know about schools in other countries?** Discuss. Then listen and read. ⌂ **039**

The Nenets people are from Western Siberia. Some Nenets live in towns and villages, but many are nomadic. Nomadic people move from place to place. Nomadic Nenets follow their reindeer herds and travel around Siberia all year. They live in camps. Some Nenets children travel with their families and learn at a special nomadic school. Teachers travel with the families and the classrooms are in the camps. Some **lessons** are the same as lessons at normal schools, but in other lessons the children also learn about Nenets traditions and skills.

At an elementary school in South Korea, children have got a new English **language** teacher. It's a robot. A teacher in Australia looks into a **camera** and speaks. In their classroom in South Korea, the children hear the teacher's voice and see her face on the robot's **screen**. They follow her **instructions** and **practise** their English.

In Bangladesh, it is often difficult for children to get to school because there are problems with heavy rain. But thousands of students now have their lessons at 'floating schools'. It is easy for these students to go to school even in bad weather because 'floating schools' are on boats. There are also floating **libraries**, with a lot of books and **laptops**.

What's your classroom like? Do you get your **homework** from a robot? Do you travel with your **classmates** to a different place every week? Do you learn on the land or on the water?

A Nenets boy studying outside his winter camp in Western Siberia

2 **LEARN NEW WORDS Listen and repeat.** 🔊040

3 **Work in pairs.** Why do you think schools have robot teachers in South Korea? Would you like to learn from a robot teacher? Why or why not?

4 Read and write the words from the list.

camera	classmate	language	laptops
lessons	library	practise	screen

Dave and Amy Freeman are National Geographic adventurers and educators. Their Wilderness Classrooms teach children about the wild and exciting places they explore. The explorers record their adventures on a _____ . Students then watch their videos on a _____ in the classroom. They can use _____ to

send questions to the explorers. Sometimes they choose the explorers' route for the next week. The _____ help children to _____ maths, geography and science skills.

Dave and Amy Freeman dogsledding in winter

5 LEARN NEW WORDS Listen to these words and match them to their opposite meanings. Then listen and repeat. 🎧 041 042

different	easy
difficult	same

6 YOU DECIDE Choose an activity.

1. **Work independently.** Write three different things you want to learn at school. Explain why you want to learn about them.

2. **Work in pairs.** Design a robot teacher. Think about what it looks like and what it can do. Draw a picture of it.

3. **Work in groups.** Imagine you can choose next week's journey for Dave and Amy Freeman. What's their route?

Talking about likes and dislikes

Which subjects do you **like**?	I **like** science, but I **don't like** maths.
Do you like PE?	Yes, I do. I **love** it.
Do you like art?	No, I don't. I **hate** it.

1 **Listen.** How do the speakers talk about their likes and dislikes? Write the phrases you hear. 🎧 044

2 **Read and complete the dialogue.**

Ahmed: What's your favourite subject at school, Haider?

Haider: _____ geography and art. How about you? Which subjects _____ ?

Ahmed: I like art, but _____ geography. I think my favourite subject is maths.

Haider: Maths? Really? _____ maths! I'm not very good at it.

Ahmed: _____ science?

Haider: _____ . Science is really interesting. Do you like science?

Ahmed: _____ . It's difficult!

3 **Work in pairs.** Spin the wheel. Tell your partner about your likes and dislikes. Then ask about your partner's likes and dislikes.

> I like the colours blue and black. I don't like the colour red. What colours do you like?

> I like yellow and green.

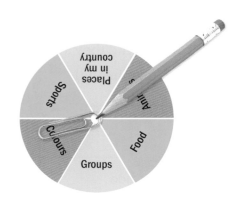

Go to page 171.

Present simple: Talking about routines, habits and permanent states

Camila **lives** in Quito.

She **gets up** at six o'clock in the morning.

I **walk** to school with her.

Her brothers **don't walk** to school. They **go** by bus.

She **doesn't have** lunch at school. She **goes** home for lunch.

She **hangs out with** with her friends after lunch.

What time **does** she **go** to bed? At half past nine.

1 **Listen.** Kerem describes a typical day in his life. Circle the correct form of the verbs you hear. ⌒046

1. get up	gets up	6. doesn't have	don't have
2. eat	eats	7. make	makes
3. doesn't have	don't have	8. return	returns
4. drink	drinks	9. finish	finishes
5. go	goes	10. do	does

2 **Read.** Complete the sentences with the correct form of the verbs in brackets.

Danilo is 12 years old and he _____ (live) in Manila in the Philippines, with his sisters, Lilybeth and Tala, and his parents. He _____ (get up) every morning at seven o'clock and he _____ (prepare) breakfast for his family. After breakfast, he _____ (start) his lessons. Danilo _____ (not go) to school. His mother _____ (teach) him at home in the morning. In the afternoon, he _____ (walk) to a music lesson at his friend's house. There are five children in the music lesson and they all _____ (practise) together. Lilybeth and Tala _____ (not go) to the music lesson. They _____ (stay) at home and _____ (study) maths or science.

LEARN NEW WORDS Listen to learn about a typical school day in Japan. Then listen and repeat. 🎧 **047 048**

School starts at 8.30 **on weekdays**.

The head teacher talks to the school **once a week**.

Lesson	Time	Monday	Tuesday	Wednesday	Thursday	Friday
	08.30	Head teacher talks to the school	Class register	Class register	Class register	Class register
1	08.45	PE	maths	geography	maths	PE
2	09.45	science	geography	science	art	science
3	10.45	art	history	art	history	geography
4	11.45	history	PE	history	PE	history
	12.30	lunch	lunch	lunch	lunch	lunch
5	1.30	maths	science	maths	science	maths
	2.30		After-school club		After-school club	

There are five lessons **every day**.

After-school clubs meet **twice a week** at the end of the school day.

There is no school **at the weekend**.

④ **Work in pairs.** Describe your typical school week. What do you do every day? What do you do once or twice a week after school? What do you do at the weekend?

⑤ **Work in groups.** Design a timetable for your ideal school. Then tell another group about your timetable.

At our school, we start lessons at half past ten every morning. We play football four times a week, and we have a maths lesson once a week.

1 BEFORE YOU READ **Discuss in pairs.** Look at the title and the photos. What do you think the reading is about?

2 LEARN NEW WORDS **Find these words in the reading.** Which words are verbs? Which word is an adjective? Then listen and repeat. ∩ 049

| fail | hard-working | improve | succeed |

1. What does Eduardo Briceño want to find out about chess champions or people who are brilliant at music or maths?
2. How does Josh Waitzkin first learn to play chess?
3. Why is his first national chess championship important for Josh?
4. What other activity is Josh also very good at?

GROWTH
MINDSET

HOW TO BE BRILLIANT

Eduardo Briceño is an expert in education. He wants to find out why some people are chess champions or brilliant at music or maths. He believes that it is because of how they think. He calls this their 'growth mindset'. These people don't believe they are special or better than other people. They believe they can work hard and improve their skills.

One example of this is Josh Waitzkin. Let's look back at his story.

When Josh is six years old, he sees people playing chess in Washington Square Park in New York City. He learns to play chess with them. He loves the game and he plays a lot of chess! He becomes very good at it. But then, a couple of years later, he loses his first national championship.

This is an important moment for Josh. He realises that it's not about how clever you are. It's about how hard you work. He works very hard and he wins the next national championship.

Then, when he is 21 years old, Josh decides to learn something completely different. He joins a Tai Chi class. Josh works very hard again and he wins a world championship!

Josh is a great example of 'growth mindset'. He doesn't believe that he is naturally good at one special thing. He tries to learn new things. He doesn't always succeed immediately, but he is very hard-working. He thinks that it's good to fail sometimes because it makes you try harder.

We can all use 'growth mindset'. Don't think that you are good at a subject or bad at a subject. Think about how you can work hard and get better at everything you do.

Josh Waitzkin doing Tai Chi

5 **Work in pairs.** What's the main idea of this reading? Underline the correct answer.

1. You can improve if you work hard.
2. Some people are very good at subjects like maths, music or chess.
3. Chess can help you to be good at other subjects.

6 **Discuss in groups.**

1. Think of a school subject that is difficult for you. How can you improve? Share your ideas.
2. Do you think people are good at things without trying? Why or why not?
3. Eduardo Briceño says, 'Mindset affects all of us.' What do you think he means?

1 **BEFORE YOU WATCH** **Discuss in pairs.** Look at the photo and guess. Where are the children going? How often do they make this journey?

2 **Work in pairs.** You're going to watch *Education Around the World*. From the title and the photo, predict which topics the video is about. Tick your predictions.

_____ age when students start school

_____ school uniform

_____ journey to/from school

_____ lunch breaks

_____ lessons

_____ school holidays

_____ teachers

_____ size of school

3 **WHILE YOU WATCH** **Check your predictions from Activity 2.** Watch scene 2.1.

4 **AFTER YOU WATCH** **Work in pairs.** Tick T for *True* or F for *False*.

1. Students in Finland begin school at the age of seven. Ⓣ Ⓕ

2. In Finland, students usually get a lot of homework. Ⓣ Ⓕ

3. Some students in Pennsylvania, USA, go to school by horse and cart. Ⓣ Ⓕ

4. Lunch breaks in French schools are usually very short. Ⓣ Ⓕ

5. The main summer holidays in Argentina begin in February. Ⓣ Ⓕ

6. Australian students have four school holidays every year. Ⓣ Ⓕ

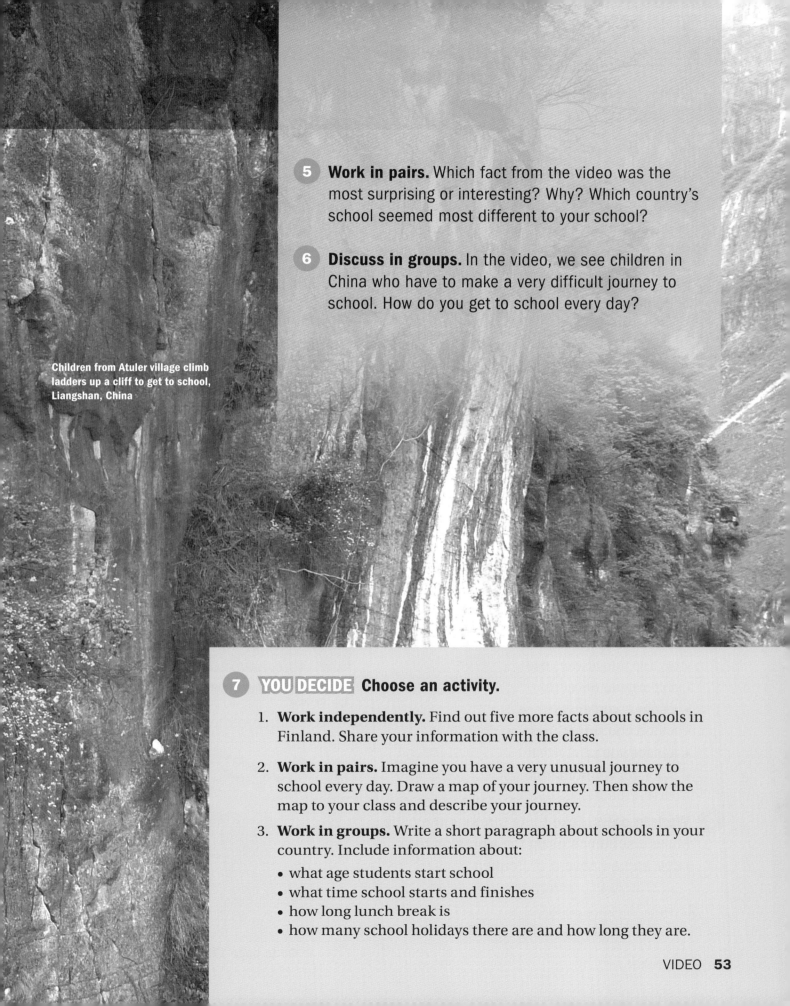

Children from Atuler village climb ladders up a cliff to get to school, Liangshan, China

5 **Work in pairs.** Which fact from the video was the most surprising or interesting? Why? Which country's school seemed most different to your school?

6 **Discuss in groups.** In the video, we see children in China who have to make a very difficult journey to school. How do you get to school every day?

7 **YOU DECIDE** **Choose an activity.**

1. **Work independently.** Find out five more facts about schools in Finland. Share your information with the class.

2. **Work in pairs.** Imagine you have a very unusual journey to school every day. Draw a map of your journey. Then show the map to your class and describe your journey.

3. **Work in groups.** Write a short paragraph about schools in your country. Include information about:
   - what age students start school
   - what time school starts and finishes
   - how long lunch break is
   - how many school holidays there are and how long they are.

Adverbs of frequency: Saying how often you do something

0% ——————————————————————→ 100%

never   rarely   sometimes   often   always

I **never** say mean things to other people.

I **rarely** forget to do my homework.

He **sometimes** gets up at six o'clock in the morning.

She **often** has lunch at school.

We **always** report bullying to an adult.

---

1 **Read.** Circle the correct adverbs of frequency.

Cyberbullying – saying bad things to or about people online – is a big problem. Of course, we should *never / sometimes* post mean things online. But it is *rarely / sometimes* difficult, especially for young people. They can be very impulsive. That means they *often / never* make decisions very quickly without thinking about them carefully first. But now there is a new app called 'ReThink'. The app *always / sometimes* checks your messages before you post them. If a message is mean, the app asks, 'Do you really want to write this?' When people stop and think about a mean message, they *rarely / always* decide to post it.

Trisha Prabhu, the inventor of the anti-cyberbullying app 'ReThink'

2 **Work in pairs.** Discuss:

- a website you often visit
- an app you always use
- a sport you never do
- a colour you always see
- a food you sometimes eat
- a place you rarely visit
- a person you sometimes see

3 **Work in pairs.** Take turns throwing the cube. Make a sentence using the words on the cube and an adverb of frequency.

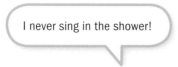

I never sing in the shower!

Go to page 175.

WRITING

When we write about a person's daily routine, we use sequencing words to show the order of events:

first   **then**   **next**   **before**   **after**

1 **Read the model.** How does the writer show the order of events? Underline the sequencing words.

A Day in My Life

On weekdays, I always get up at half past six in the morning. First, I have a shower, and then I have breakfast with my family. Next, I go to school. My family lives on a small island and I always go to school by boat! When the weather is very bad, I stay at home and my teacher sends me extra homework by email. School starts at 8.45 and lunch is at twelve o'clock. I often have rice with fish. After lunch, we have music or art. School finishes at three o'clock, but once a week, on Wednesday afternoon, I stay at school for football club. I really love football! I get home at four o'clock. I often go swimming in the sea before supper, and then I do my homework. I go to bed at nine o'clock. The stars are very beautiful and I can hear the sea.

2 **Work in pairs.** How similar is the writer's typical day to your day? Which things are the same? Which things are different?

3 **Write.** Describe a day in your life. Use sequencing words.

Believe in Yourself

'At one point I was a student sitting in a classroom just like them and I wanted to be an explorer. And now I am! And they can do it, too, if they want to.'

Dave Freeman

Dave and Amy Freeman
National Geographic Explorers, Adventurers and Educators

1. Watch scene 2.2.

2. Dave and Amy Freeman travel around the world and tell children about their experiences. What do you think the children learn from their adventures?

3. Do you want to be an explorer? Why or why not?

Make an Impact

YOU DECIDE Choose a project.

1 **Design your perfect school.**

· Think about the classroom, the timetable and the lessons.

· Make an advertisement for your school.

· Present your advertisement to your classmates. Do they want to join your school?

2 **Plan and do a video interview.**

· Find out about a typical school day in another country.

· Imagine you are a student in that country. Film a role-play interview about your day with a classmate.

· Show your video to your classmates and answer their questions.

3 **Make a school guide for new students.**

· Write down the most important facts about your school.

· Draw a map to show where the different classrooms are.

· Put the information together to make a leaflet about your school for new students.

Express Yourself

1 **Read and listen to the text messages about World Food Day.** 🎧 **052**

Hi, Mum. It's World Food Day at school tomorrow! Help! I have to bring some typical food from Japan. 😊

Tomorrow??

Yes, tomorrow. Sorry! The note about it is in my bag. 😣 Have you got any ideas for a typical dish from Japan?

What about some sushi? That's a typical Japanese food and it's easy to make.

That's a great idea! Can you get the ingredients for me this afternoon, please? Then we can make it when I get home from school. 😄

I'm at work this afternoon, but Grandad is always happy to help. You know he's good at cooking! You can go to the supermarket together after school.

Cool. What do we need?

You need some rice, some seaweed, a cucumber, some fish, some soy sauce and some ginger.

OK. Thanks, Mum.

Good luck making sushi!

Maki sushi

2 **Work in groups.** Discuss the text messages.

1. What do you think students learn about at World Food Day?

2. Imagine it's World Food Day at your school. You can make a dish from any country in the world. Which country do you choose? What dish do you make?

3 **Connect ideas.** In Unit 1, you learnt about food and families. In Unit 2, you learnt about education. What connection do you see between the two units?

4 **YOU DECIDE** **Choose an activity.**

1. Choose a topic:
   - a family celebration
   - a school celebration

2. Choose a way to express yourself:
   - an online conversation
   - an email
   - a recipe

3. Present your work.

Robots and Us

'We know that robots are going to have an impact on society.'

Chad Jenkins

A robot at work at the Institute of Robotics and Mechatronics, Germany

TO START

1. Look at the photo. What is the robot doing? What else do you think this robot can do?

2. Would you like to have a robot in your home? Why or why not?

3. Think about your home. How many machines are there? What jobs do they do? What would your life be like without them?

What do you think of when you hear the word 'robot'? Perhaps you imagine something that **follows** our instructions, brings us our clothes and **helps** us around the home. These robots do exist, but scientists also **design** many other kinds of robots for other important jobs.

Doctors use medical robots for surgery. They can use the robots to make very careful movements. The doctors can even **control** the robots from far away. Other doctors also use another type of robot – a therapy robot. One type of therapy robot called Paro looks and acts like a baby seal. It has got a movable head and flippers. When patients hold this robot, they feel relaxed and happy. Sometimes their **pain** levels improve.

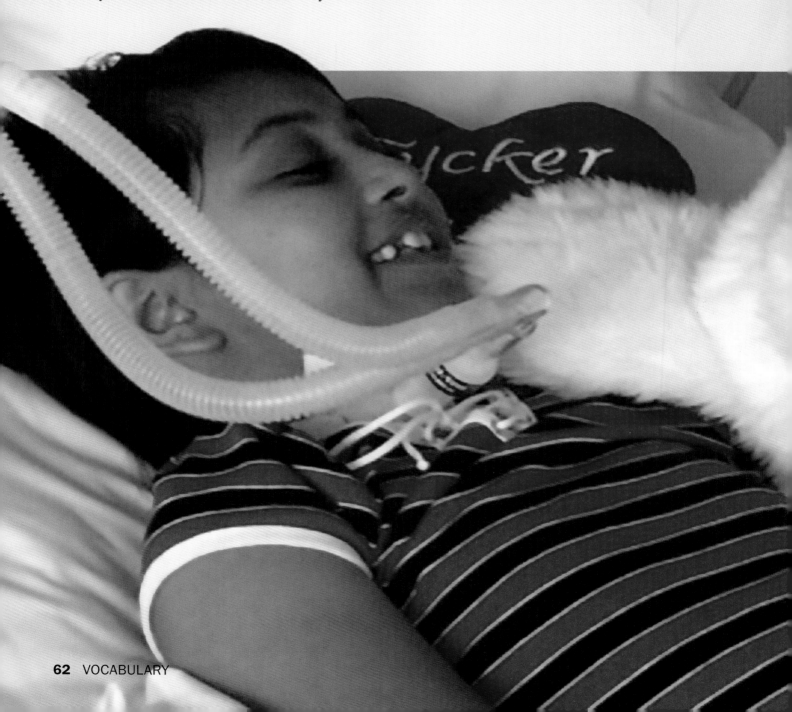

Explorers **send** robot vehicles to places that are difficult to reach, for example, deep below the sea. They can watch the robots on a screen and control them **online** using their keyboard and **mouse**. They can decide where and when the robots move. People also use robots to do very dangerous jobs. For example, if there is a fire in a building, a robot can go into the building and look for people.

In factories, robots do a lot of very **boring** assembly line jobs. When humans do repetitive jobs – the same thing, again and again – they can make mistakes, but robots don't get bored.

A robot rescue vehicle, Russia

A child in hospital cuddling Paro, a life-like baby seal robot, Japan

2 **LEARN NEW WORDS** Listen and repeat. 🎧054

3 **Work in pairs.** Design a therapy robot. What does it look like? What does it do? How does it make people feel happy? Share your ideas with the class.

4 **Read and write the words from the list.** Make any necessary changes.

control	design	doctor	follow	help	online	send

Chad Jenkins is a computer scientist and roboticist. He _____ robots.
He wants to teach his robots how to learn new things. A lot of people _____
Chad to teach his robots. They visit Chad's robot lab _____ . Then they
_____ instructions to the robots. The robots _____
the instructions. People who visit Chad's lab _____ the robots online.
They can tell the robots to play football or to do some household chores. The robots learn new
things and improve because they get a lot of practice.

5 **LEARN NEW WORDS Listen to these words and match them to their definitions.** Then listen and repeat. 🎧 055 056

bring	hold	movable	move

_____ 1. change from one
position to another

_____ 2. have something in your
hands or arms

_____ 3. take something or
someone with you to
a place

_____ 4. able to change position

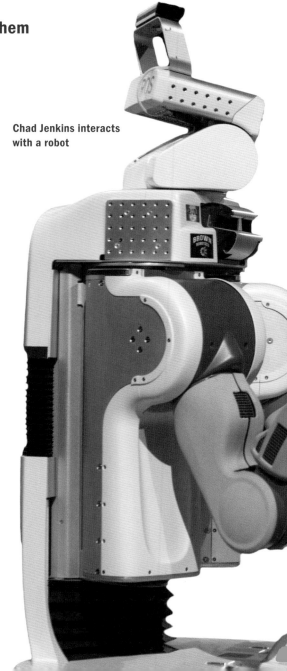

Chad Jenkins interacts with a robot

6 **YOU DECIDE** **Choose an activity.**

1. **Work independently.** Write a list of five instructions
for the robots in Chad Jenkins' lab.

2. **Work in pairs.** Henry Evans works with Chad.
He can't speak or move his arms or legs. Think of
different ways a robot might help Henry.

3. **Work in groups.** Think of a very simple task for a
robot, for example, 'Bring me my book.' or 'Check
my email.' Then write instructions for every
step of the task.

Reacting

That's amazing!	That's boring!
That's fantastic!	That's a bit weird!
That's so cool!	That's scary!

1 **Listen.** How do the speakers react? Write the phrases you hear. 🎧 058

2 **Read and complete the dialogue.**

Krish: There's an article in this magazine about robots.

Mariana: Robots! _____

Krish: No, it isn't! It's really interesting. This robot looks like a baby seal.

Mariana: Wow! _____

Krish: They even use them in hospitals.

Mariana: In hospitals? _____

Krish: Not really. The robots help patients to feel happy and relaxed.

Mariana: Really? _____

3 **Work in pairs.** Pick a card and react to the information on it.

DogBot is a robot dog. It can understand voice commands.

Go to page 177.

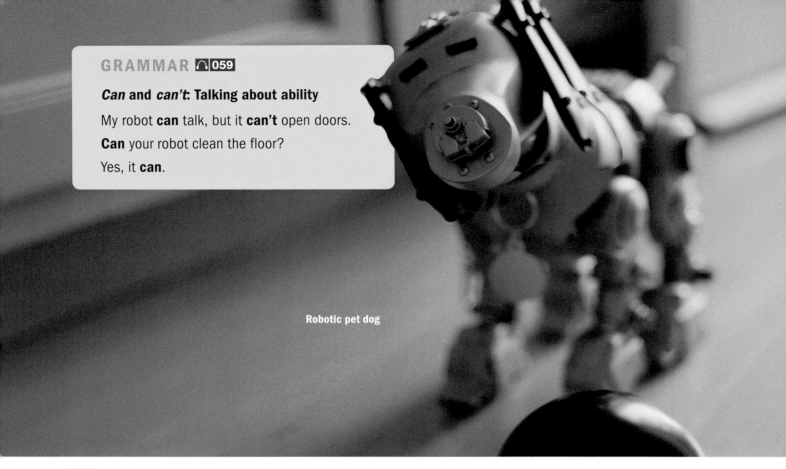

GRAMMAR 🎧 059

***Can* and *can't*: Talking about ability**

My robot **can** talk, but it **can't** open doors.

Can your robot clean the floor?

Yes, it **can**.

Robotic pet dog

1 **Listen.** Tick the correct answers. 🎧 060

	can	can't
jump		✓
walk		
run		
load the dishwasher		

	can	can't
go upstairs		
dance		
talk		
understand voice instructions		

2 **Work in pairs.** Imagine you have got a robot. Think of five things it can do and five things it can't do. You can use the ideas in the box below or your own ideas. Then compare your robot with another pair's robot.

hold things	run	jump	swim	talk
laugh	sing	load the dishwasher	clean the house	play football
dance	drive a car	read a book	understand voice instructions	

> Our robot can hold things and it can dance, but it can't sing. Can your robot sing?

> Yes, it can. Our robot can sing and it can run, but it can't understand voice instructions.

3 **LEARN NEW WORDS Listen to learn about what robots can and can't do.** Then listen and repeat. 🎧 061 062

Robots can't **imagine** things.

Humans can feel sad and **cry**.

Humans can feel happy and **laugh**.

Robots can't **dream**.

4 **Work in pairs.** Complete these sentences about yourself. Then compare your answers with your partner.

I sometimes dream about …

I laugh when …

I like to imagine I'm …

I cry when …

5 **Work in groups.** What do you think these robots can do? What can't they do? Complete the sentences below with your own ideas.

A fast-food restaurant robot _can prepare food and it can do the washing up. It can talk to people. It can't laugh and it can't use a computer._

A hospital robot _____

_____

A school robot _____

_____

A police robot _____

_____

Girls Can Code

1 BEFORE YOU READ Discuss in pairs. Look at the title and the photo. What do you think the reading is about?

2 LEARN NEW WORDS Find these words in the reading. Use the other words around them to guess their meaning. Then listen and repeat. 🎧 063

code	program
engineering	project

3 WHILE YOU READ Think about the main point of each paragraph. 🎧 064

4 AFTER YOU READ Look at the sentences. Tick T for *True* or F for *False*.

1. Boys aren't better than girls at maths and science at school.

2. Many girls study computer science at university.

3. Reshma Saujani works as an engineer.

4. 'Girls Who Code' is an after-school club organisation.

5. Girls can make computers at 'Girls Who Code' clubs.

6. A lot of girls want to study computer science or engineering at university because of 'Girls Who Code' clubs. Ⓣ Ⓕ

How to Change the Future

Boys and girls are both good at science and maths at school. But there is a big 'gender divide' in subjects like computer science and engineering at university. A 'gender divide' means there is a difference between what girls do and what boys do. Very few girls study computer science or engineering at university and very few girls get jobs in these subject areas. In fact, only 20% of engineering graduates and only 18% of computer science graduates in the USA are girls.

Computer science and engineering are useful and interesting subjects. Engineers use science and maths to create and design things. Computer scientists work on new computer programs. So how can we get more girls to study these subjects?

Reshma Saujani is an American lawyer. She wants to change things. Her organisation, 'Girls Who Code', runs after-school clubs and summer schools all around the USA. The clubs are free, and they teach girls how to write code, or special instructions, for computers. The girls use these instructions to make basic computer programs. They work on projects together to help their community.

The clubs are a big success. There are now 10,000 girls in 'Girls Who Code' after-school clubs around the USA. Many of these girls want to study computer science or engineering when they leave school.

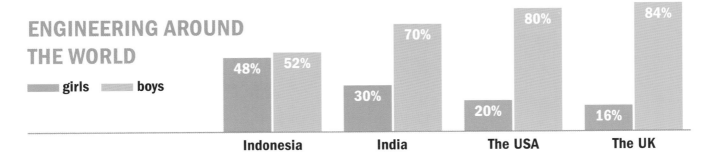

ENGINEERING AROUND THE WORLD

girls   boys

	Indonesia	India	The USA	The UK
girls	48%	30%	20%	16%
boys	52%	70%	80%	84%

5 **Work in pairs.** Write the correct paragraph number for the descriptions below.

_____ An explanation of computer science and engineering.

_____ The effect of the 'Girls Who Code' clubs.

_____ An introduction to the topic.

_____ A description of the 'Girls Who Code' clubs.

6 **Discuss in groups.**

1. Do you think there are any subjects that girls are better at or that boys are better at? Why or why not?

2. Why do you think STEM subjects (science, technology, engineering and maths) are less popular with girls? How can we change that?

3. Imagine you can organise some after-school clubs around your area. What clubs do you want to organise? Why do you want to organise these clubs? Who will join them?

VIDE▶

1 **BEFORE YOU WATCH Discuss in pairs.** How can robots help explorers in places that are very dangerous or difficult to reach?

2 **Work in pairs.** You are going to watch *Squishy Robot Fingers*. Before you watch, look at the photo. What do you think it shows? What is it doing?

3 **WHILE YOU WATCH Check your answers from Activity 2.** Were they correct? What else did you learn about Squishy Fingers? Watch scene 3.1.

4 **AFTER YOU WATCH Work in pairs.** Circle the correct words.

1. David Gruber first tested Squishy Fingers in a *swimming pool / coral reef* .

2. Now he is testing it *in a boat / on a coral reef* .

3. Squishy Fingers is made from *metal / rubber* .

4. David's old robots were designed for *coral / oil exploration* .

5. Squishy Fingers grabs a *small / large* piece of coral.

6. David and the team are *happy / unhappy* with the test.

5 **Work in pairs.** Compare Squishy Fingers' hands with the older robot hands. Draw a table with three headings: *Task*, *Squishy Fingers* and *Older Robot Hands*. Tick which robot could do each task better.

Squishy Fingers in action underwater

6 Work in groups. Think of ways to use robots to explore the places listed below. How would you change the robot for each place?

a volcano   the Sahara desert

the Arctic   an underground cave

7 YOU DECIDE Choose an activity.

1. **Work independently.** David Gruber is an underwater explorer. In the video, he uses Squishy Fingers to collect a piece of coral in the ocean. Where else could Squishy Fingers work? Make a list of your ideas.

2. **Work in pairs.** Design an advert for Squishy Fingers. Include information about what it can do. Make a video or perform your advert to the class.

3. **Work in groups.** Find out about another piece of equipment used in underwater exploration. Write a short description of the equipment and what it does. Tell the class about it.

Should and **shouldn't**: Giving advice

We **should** join the after-school coding club.

You **shouldn't** buy this robot. It's very expensive.

They **should** study for this maths test.

1 **Read.** Use *should* or *shouldn't* with the correct verb from the box to complete the sentences.

| forget | join | learn | look | read | spend | start | study | watch |

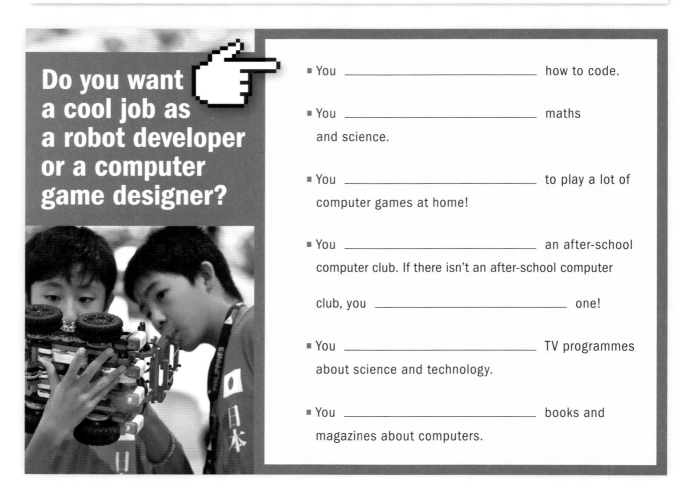

Do you want a cool job as a robot developer or a computer game designer?

- You _____ how to code.

- You _____ maths and science.

- You _____ to play a lot of computer games at home!

- You _____ an after-school computer club. If there isn't an after-school computer club, you _____ one!

- You _____ TV programmes about science and technology.

- You _____ books and magazines about computers.

2 **Work in pairs.** Take turns. Choose a card. Read the sentence. Ask your partner for advice.

You should ask your maths teacher for help.

I don't understand my maths homework.

Go to page 179.

WRITING

When we contrast two different things, we use words like *but* and *however*.
We can use *however* at the beginning of a sentence.

> *Your robot is very strong,* **but** *it isn't very intelligent.*
> *My robot cleans the floor.* **However,** *it can't open the door.*

1 **Read the model.** How does the writer contrast information? Underline the words that show contrast.

Buddy and Sega™ Toys Dream Cat are both robots, but they're very different. Buddy is a companion robot. He's got three wheels and he's got a screen for a face. However, he hasn't got moveable arms, so he can't bring things to you and he can't wash your dishes! He can check your emails and he can wake you up in the morning, but he's very expensive. Sega™ Toys Dream Cat is a robot pet. She can't check your emails or wake you up in the morning, but she is very cute! She can purr and she can move her tail. However, she can't walk or run. Which robot do you prefer?

Buddy the robot

Sega™ Toys Dream Cat

2 **Work in pairs.** Find two things Buddy can do and two things he can't do. Find two things Sega™ Toys Dream Cat can do and two things she can't do.

3 **Write.** Compare two different gadgets in your house, for example, a smartphone and a computer. Think about what they're like, what they can do and what they can't do. Use *but* and *however* to show contrast.

NATIONAL GEOGRAPHIC

Change the World

'We provide the technology so that you can help us to reach out and change the world.'

Chad Jenkins

National Geographic Explorer, Computer Scientist and Roboticist

1. Watch scene 3.2.

2. Chad Jenkins develops new types of robots. How do you think they can help change the world?

3. Imagine you can use technology to change your town or country. What technology do you use? How does it change your town or country?

Make an Impact

1 **Prepare a presentation about a famous robot.**

· Find out facts about a famous robot – fictional or real.

· Find photos and illustrations of the robot.

· Give a presentation about the robot to the class.

2 **Design your own robot.**

· Think about what your robot can and can't do.

· Draw a picture of your robot and label it.

· Display your picture in the class. Answer your classmates' questions about it.

3 **Write a Coding Club Invitation.**

· Decide when the club will be and what students will learn.

· Include information about why learning to code is important.

· Send your Coding Club Invitation to your classmates.

C-3PO and R2D2 from *Star Wars: Episode III Revenge of the Sith*

Part of Nature

Butterflies on the shoreline of the
Juruena River, Brazil

'We are part of nature and the ecosystem, not something separate.'
Juliana Machado Ferreira

TO START

1. Look at the photo and read the caption. What kinds of animals live in this place? Would you visit here? Why or why not?

2. How are you 'part of nature'? What do you think nature and wild animals can teach us?

3. Do you sometimes visit zoos or wildlife parks? Which animals do you see there?

Did you know that almost 7,000 different types of animals are **endangered**? Fortunately, there are some amazing wildlife **conservation** projects around the world.

Thanks to conservation projects, giant **pandas** are not endangered anymore, but they still need our help. There are now 1,800 pandas in the **wild**, and the panda population is growing slowly. Thirty per cent of the world's population of giant pandas lives in the Sichuan Giant Panda Sanctuaries in China. These sanctuaries are famous for their work with giant pandas and with other endangered animals, including snow leopards and red pandas.

There are seven nature reserves in a very big **area** of land in the sanctuaries. Here, giant pandas can live safely in the wild. Their favourite food, bamboo, **grows** in the **forests** around the mountains.

Increasing the giant panda population is a very important part of the sanctuaries' conservation work. At a special research centre, **workers** keep some pandas in **captivity** for breeding. When the baby pandas are born, the workers help the mothers to look after them. They try to teach them how to live in the wild. They don't want the pandas to be too friendly with people, so the workers wear panda **costumes**!

With a combination of conservation, research, science and some very cute costumes, the Sichuan Giant Panda Sanctuaries are continuing to help to bring giant pandas back into the wild.

A worker wearing a panda costume,
Wolong, Sichuan Province, China

2 LEARN NEW WORDS **Listen and repeat.** 🎧 067

3 **Work in pairs.** Why do you think the workers don't want the baby pandas to be too friendly with people?

4 Read and write the words from the list.

| area | captivity | conservation | endangered | forest | wild | worker |

National Geographic Explorer Juliana Machado Ferreira is a conservation biologist. She works on _____ projects in Brazil. There is a big problem in Brazil because people take _____ birds from their homes in the _____ and then sell them as pets. Because of this, some of these birds are now _____ .
Juliana wants to teach people that when you keep these birds in _____ , it's very bad for nature. She uses her knowledge of biology to find out which _____ the birds originally come from, and then she returns the birds to their homes.

Juliana Machado Ferreira

5 LEARN NEW WORDS Listen to these words and match them to their definitions. Then listen and repeat. 🎧 068 069

| leopard | mountain | reserve | wildlife |

_____ 1. a place where the animals and plants are protected

_____ 2. animals and plants that live in a natural environment

_____ 3. a large wild animal of the cat family

_____ 4. a very high hill

6 YOU DECIDE Choose an activity.

1. **Work independently.** Why is it a bad idea to own a wild animal as a pet? Think of three reasons. Share your ideas with the class.

2. **Work in pairs.** Imagine you work at the Sichuan Giant Panda Sanctuaries research centre. What do you like about your work? What parts of your work are difficult?

3. **Work in groups.** Design an advertisement for the Sichuan Giant Panda Sanctuaries.

Checking facts

There are seven nature reserves in the Sichuan Giant Panda Sanctuaries.	**Really**?
Yes. The most famous is the Wolong Nature Reserve.	**How big** is it?
It's 2,000 square kilometres.	**How many** pandas are there?
I don't know exactly. I think there are about 100.	**Are there really** 100 pandas there?
I think so!	

1 **Listen.** How do the speakers check information? Write the phrases you hear. 🎧 071

2 **Read and complete the dialogue.**

Samira: Hey, look at these cute baby panda pictures! They're from the research centre in Sichuan, China. The workers wear panda costumes.

Hadil: _____ ?

Samira: Yes, look!

Hadil: _____ baby pandas are at the research centre?

Samira: There are 16 babies.

Hadil: _____ 16 baby pandas there?

Samira: Yes, there are. It's a very successful centre.

Hadil: _____ is it?

Samira: I don't know, but the Sichuan Giant Panda Sanctuaries reserve is very big. It covers 9,245 square kilometres.

3 **Work in pairs.** Take turns. Choose an information card. Give the matching picture card to your partner. Answer your partner's questions about the nature reserve on your information card.

Yala National Park
- Where: Sri Lanka
- Size: 979 square kilometres
- Number of elephants: 350
- Other animals: leopards, bears and buffalo

Go to page 181.

Quantifiers: Talking and asking about quantity

How many different kinds of camels are there?

There are two kinds of camels.

How much food do they eat every day?

A lot! Camels eat **a lot** of cacti and dry plants.

There is very **little** grass and there are very **few** plants in the desert.

1 **Read.** Use *how much, how many, a lot, little* and *few* to complete the fact sheet.

Camels: FAQs

_____ humps has a camel got?

Well, it depends. Dromedary camels have got one hump and Bactrian camels have got two humps.

_____ water can a camel drink?

_____ ! There is very _____ water in the desert.

When a camel finds water, it can drink _____ !

_____ wild Bactrian camels are there in the world?

There are very _____ wild Bactrian camels. There are only about
1,000 in the wild. They are endangered.

2 **Work in pairs.** Write two more questions about camels with *how much* or *how many*.
Then do some research to find out the answers. Share your answers with the class.

How _____?

How _____?

**An Afar camel caravan crosses the
salt flats of Lake Assal, Djibouti**

3 **LEARN NEW WORDS Listen and read to learn about camels.** Then listen and repeat. 🎧 073 074

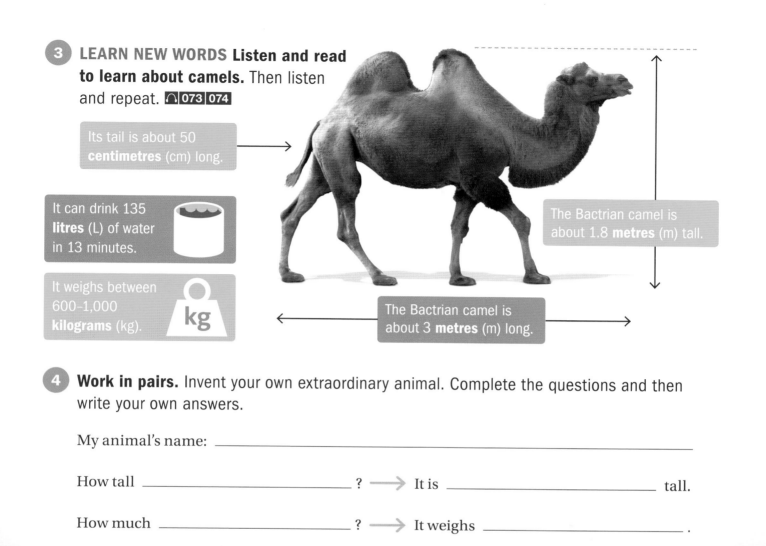

Its tail is about 50 **centimetres** (cm) long.

It can drink 135 **litres** (L) of water in 13 minutes.

It weighs between 600–1,000 **kilograms** (kg).

The Bactrian camel is about 1.8 **metres** (m) tall.

The Bactrian camel is about 3 **metres** (m) long.

4 **Work in pairs.** Invent your own extraordinary animal. Complete the questions and then write your own answers.

My animal's name: _____

How tall _____ ? ⟶ It is _____ tall.

How much _____ ? ⟶ It weighs _____ .

How much _____ ? ⟶ It drinks _____
of water in _____ minutes.

How far _____ ? ⟶ It can walk _____
in _____ day(s).

5 **Work in groups.** Ask other students about their amazing animal.

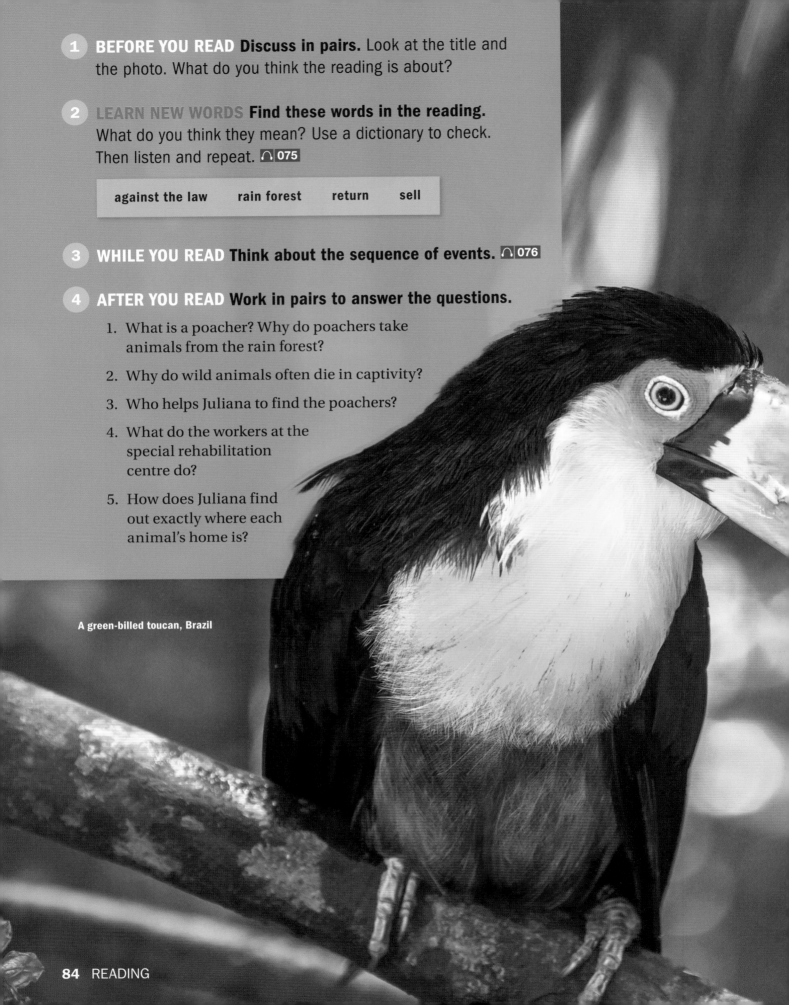

1 **BEFORE YOU READ Discuss in pairs.** Look at the title and the photo. What do you think the reading is about?

2 **LEARN NEW WORDS Find these words in the reading.** What do you think they mean? Use a dictionary to check. Then listen and repeat. ∩ 075

| against the law | rain forest | return | sell |

3 **WHILE YOU READ Think about the sequence of events.** ∩ 076

4 **AFTER YOU READ Work in pairs to answer the questions.**

1. What is a poacher? Why do poachers take animals from the rain forest?

2. Why do wild animals often die in captivity?

3. Who helps Juliana to find the poachers?

4. What do the workers at the special rehabilitation centre do?

5. How does Juliana find out exactly where each animal's home is?

A green-billed toucan, Brazil

A WILD ANIMAL ISN'T A PET

RETURNING WILD ANIMALS TO THE RAIN FOREST

Every year in Brazil, people take millions of animals from the rain forest and sell them as pets. These people are called poachers. This is against the law, but people love to buy these beautiful animals and keep them as pets. In fact, people in Brazil spend more than £1.5 billion every year on birds, turtles, lizards and other wild pets. However, the animals are not happy in captivity. People don't know how to care for them. The animals often die because they eat the wrong food or because they are very unhappy. Wild animals have an important role in nature. If people take them from their homes in the wild, it can cause problems for other wildlife.

Juliana Machado Ferreira works together with the police to find the poachers and to save the animals. She then takes them to a special centre where workers look after the animals. They teach the animals how to find food in the wild. The birds learn how to fly again. When they are ready, the animals can return to the rain forest.

Juliana now has another important job. She wants to find out exactly where each animal's home is in the rain forest. But the rain forest in Brazil is a very big place. Juliana looks at the animals' DNA. This gives her important information about each animal and its home. Then, at last, she can take the animals back to the right places in the rain forest.

5 **Work in pairs.** Put these events into the correct order.

_____ Workers at the centre help the animals to learn important skills.

_____ The animals return to the rain forest.

_____ Juliana and the police save the wild animals from the poachers.

_____ Juliana takes the wild animals to a special centre.

_____ Poachers take wild animals from the rain forest.

_____ Juliana looks at the animals' DNA.

6 **Discuss in groups.**

1. Does the reading change your opinion about wild animals as pets? Explain why or why not.
2. Why do you think it's important for the animals to return to exactly the same place in the rain forest? Think of several different reasons.
3. Do you think it's important to learn about the wild animals from your own country? Why or why not?

Discuss in pairs. What do you already know about pandas? Remember what you read about pandas on page 78. Try to answer these questions together:

1. In which country do many giant pandas live?
2. How many giant pandas are there in the wild?
3. What food do giant pandas love to eat?

A giant panda cub, Wolong, Sichuan Province, China

2 **Read and circle.** You are going to watch *Into the Real Wild: Photographing Pandas with Ami Vitale*. From the title, predict what the video is about. Circle the letter.

a. Returning pandas to the wild
b. Looking for pandas in the wild

3 **Circle the words you hear.** Watch scene 4.1.

baby	camera	captivity	costume	forest
leopard	mother	mountain	school	student

4 **AFTER YOU WATCH** **Work in pairs.** Tick T for *True* or F for *False*.

1. China takes pandas born in captivity and releases them into the wild. Ⓣ Ⓕ

2. Mother pandas go for several months without food and water after their baby is born. Ⓣ Ⓕ

3. Baby pandas grow very slowly. Ⓣ Ⓕ

4. 'Papa Panda' is the name of a very old panda at the Wolong China Conservation and Research Centre. Ⓣ Ⓕ

5. Workers at the Conservation Centre teach pandas how to live in the wild. Ⓣ Ⓕ

6. Leopards and pandas often play together at the Conservation Centre. Ⓣ Ⓕ

5 **Work in pairs.** At the beginning of the video, Ami says, 'As a National Geographic photographer, my job is to surprise people'. Which photos or facts in the video surprised you? Explain.

6 **Work in groups.** In the video, workers try to prepare pandas for life in the wild. Think about how animals survive in the wild. What do they need to do and know in order to survive? Make a list of the most important skills.

7 **YOU DECIDE** **Choose an activity.**

1. **Work independently.** What do you want to know about the life of a worker at the Wolong China Conservation and Research Centre? Write a list of questions. Then read your questions to the class and ask them to suggest possible answers.

2. **Work in pairs.** Role-play a conversation between Ami and a reporter who wants to know about her experiences in China. Share your dialogue with the class.

3. **Work in groups.** Find out about an endangered animal and ways to protect it. Share with the class.

Adverbs: Saying how you do something

Cheetahs are fast runners. They can run very **fast** at 113 kilometres per hour.

Elephants are good at swimming. They can swim very **well**.

The three-toed sloth is a slow animal. It moves very **slowly**.

The howler monkey has got a loud voice. It can call very **loudly**.

good ⟶ well   high ⟶ high   easy ⟶ easily

fast ⟶ fast   bad ⟶ badly   gentle ⟶ gently

1 **Work in pairs.** Complete the sentences with the correct form of a word from the box.

bad	easy	good	high	loud	fast	quiet

Cats can jump very _____ . They can jump five times their own height. They can run very _____ at 50 kilometres per hour. They have got good noses, and they can smell things very _____ from far away. They have also got very good ears. Even if you speak _____ , your cat can hear you! All cats meow when they are angry or hungry, but some cats are very noisy. Siamese cats are famous because they meow _____ when they are hungry. Cats are also good at climbing. It isn't difficult for them to climb trees. They can go up very _____ , but sometimes they forget how to come down again!

2 **Work in pairs.** Make sentences about the animals below and their abilities.

dogs	dolphins	pandas	parrots	snakes	tigers
climb	hear	move	run	speak	swim
easily	fast	loudly	quickly	quietly	well

3 **Work in pairs.** Play *Noughts and Crosses*. Make adverbs from the words in the grid. Use them to describe things that you can or can't do. Mark X or O. Try to get three in a row.

> I can't swim very well!

good	bad	fast
loud	quiet	slow
easy	high	quick

WRITING

When we write a fact sheet, we need to check all the facts carefully.

Separate the facts into different sections. We can separate the facts with headings or bullet points:

Diet

Parrots eat fruit, seeds and small insects.

Habitat

A lot of parrots live in the rain forest.

Fun facts

- *Parrots are often brightly coloured.*
- *There are more than 350 different types of parrot.*

Read the model. How does the writer separate the information? Underline the headings and circle the bullet points.

The Capybara

The capybara is a large hairy mammal. It's the size of a pig – about 50–60 centimetres tall and about 100–130 centimetres long. It weighs between 30 and 80 kilograms. It hasn't got a tail.

Habitat:

Capybaras are from South and Central America. They always live near water.

Diet:

Capybaras are herbivores. They eat water plants and grass. They don't eat meat.

Fun facts:

- Capybaras can swim very well. They can stay under the water for five minutes.
- Capybaras are very friendly. They usually live together in large groups.
- Capybaras are very noisy! They can make a lot of different sounds.

Work in pairs. Look at the questions about capybaras. Which ones can you answer using information from the fact sheet?

- What do they eat?
- How big are they?
- Where do they live?
- How fast can they run?
- How much do they eat?
- Do they live alone or in groups?

Write. Write a fact sheet about a different animal. Choose an animal from this unit or any other animal. Use headings and bullet points to separate the facts.

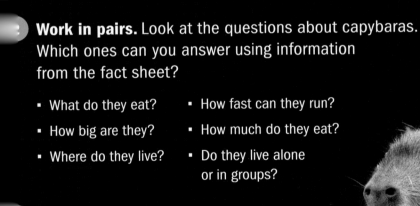

Four squirrel monkeys on a capybara

NATIONAL GEOGRAPHIC

Use Your Skills

'Do whatever is in your reach … we need to act, and act now.'

Juliana Machado Ferreira
National Geographic Explorer, Conservation Biologist

1. Watch scene 4.2.

2. Juliana talks about doing 'whatever is in your reach'. Think about Juliana's work. How does she use her special knowledge and abilities to help animals?

3. Think about some problems in your own area. How can you use your knowledge and abilities to help solve these problems?

Make an Impact

YOU DECIDE Choose a project.

1 **Plan and hold an endangered animal quiz.**

- Prepare cards with *true* or *false* sentences about endangered animals.
- Organise two teams in your class.
- Hold the quiz. Read each fact aloud. Classmates say if your sentence is true or false.

2 **Write a diary entry.**

- Imagine that you work at a wildlife reserve. Think about which animals you look after and what you do.
- Write a description of your day. Include photos.
- Show your diary entry to your classmates. Answer their questions about it.

3 **Make a wild animal poster.**

- Choose a wild animal and find out about it. Collect information and photos.
- Organise your information on a poster.
- Display your poster in the classroom. Present it to your classmates.

Golden snub-nosed monkeys

Express Yourself

1 Read and listen to the advertisement. 🎧 078

Robotosaurus Rex

This amazing remote-controlled robot dinosaur is more than a toy —

IT'S A PET AND A FRIEND!

- Clap your hands to make your dinosaur sit or stand.
- Use the remote control to make your dinosaur walk, run fast or lie down.
- Play music through the remote control to make your dinosaur dance!
- Throw the remote control and watch your dinosaur chase it.
- Look at the lights on your dinosaur's back to check its mood:

BLUE	RED	GREEN	YELLOW
happy	angry	tired	hungry

Remote control

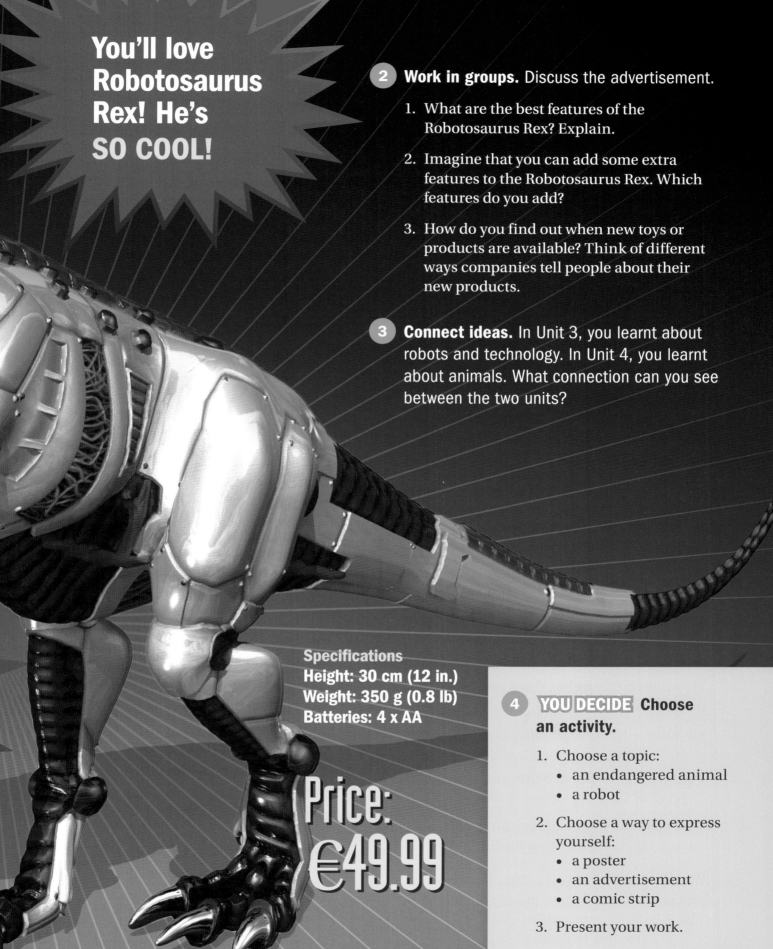

You'll love Robotosaurus Rex! He's SO COOL!

Specifications
Height: 30 cm (12 in.)
Weight: 350 g (0.8 lb)
Batteries: 4 x AA

Price:
€49.99

2 **Work in groups.** Discuss the advertisement.

1. What are the best features of the Robotosaurus Rex? Explain.

2. Imagine that you can add some extra features to the Robotosaurus Rex. Which features do you add?

3. How do you find out when new toys or products are available? Think of different ways companies tell people about their new products.

3 **Connect ideas.** In Unit 3, you learnt about robots and technology. In Unit 4, you learnt about animals. What connection can you see between the two units?

4 **YOU DECIDE** **Choose an activity.**

1. Choose a topic:
   - an endangered animal
   - a robot

2. Choose a way to express yourself:
   - a poster
   - an advertisement
   - a comic strip

3. Present your work.

Unit 1

Syllables and stress

1 **Listen.** Words in English have one or more parts. Each part is called a *syllable*. Each syllable has a vowel sound in it. It can also have one or more consonant sounds. Listen to the syllables in these words for nationalities. 🎧 **133**

1	2		3		
▢	▢	▢	▢	▢	▢
French	**Ger** - man		Kor - **e** - an		
	Spa - nish		Ja - pan - **ese**		

In words with two or more syllables, one syllable is always stronger than the other. It is pronounced loudly and more clearly. This is called the stressed syllable. Listen again and notice the stressed syllable in the two- and three-syllable words above.

2 **Listen and repeat.** Listen to these words for nationalities. How many syllables do they have? Write *2* or *3* for the number of syllables. 🎧 **134**

1. Taiwanese ___3___
2. English _____
3. Chilean _____
4. Indian _____
5. Chinese _____
6. Russian _____

3 **Work in pairs.** Listen again and repeat the words. Underline the stressed syllable in each word. 🎧 **135**

Unit 2

The third person -s and -es endings

1 **Listen.** Notice the different pronunciation of the -s ending of these three verbs. 🎧 **136**

writes   plays   teaches

The -s verb ending has three possible pronunciations:

- a soft *s* after words ending in -p, -t, -k and -f
- a hard *z* after words ending in -b, -d, -g, -l, -r, -w, -m, -n, -v and -y
- an *iz* sound after words ending in -s, -ch, -sh, -ge, -ss, -x and -z

We use exactly the same rules for the pronunciation of regular plural nouns.

2 **Listen and repeat.** Then write the words in the correct column. 🎧 **137**

crashes	gives	jumps	learns
misses	~~plays~~	runs	sits
speaks	~~teaches~~	watches	~~writes~~

soft *s*	hard *z*	*iz* sound
writes	plays	teaches

3 **Work in pairs.** Listen and repeat the sentences. Make sure you pronounce the verb endings correctly. 🎧 **138**

1. Josh studies chess every day.
2. Josh wins a chess championship.
3. Then he loses an important game of chess.
4. He decides to learn a new sport.
5. He thinks it is good to fail sometimes.

Unit 3

The *th* sound

1 **Listen.** Notice the two different ways we pronounce the letters *th*. 🎧**139**

these, those

three, thousand

- The *th* sound in *these* and *those* is voiced. It is a harder sound.

- The *th* sound in *three* and *thousand* is unvoiced. It is a softer sound.

2 **Listen and repeat.** Decide if you hear an unvoiced *th* like *three* or a voiced *th* like *these*. Write *U* for unvoiced or *V* for voiced. 🎧**140**

1. brother   V
2. the   _____
3. birthday   _____
4. that   _____
5. nothing   _____
6. month   _____
7. father   _____
8. thing   _____

3 **Work in pairs.** Listen and repeat the sentences. Make sure you pronounce the *th* sounds correctly. 🎧**141**

1. I think that boy is your brother.
2. My father's birthday is next month.
3. This is a therapy robot.
4. The maths club at my school is on Thursday.
5. There is something in the bath!

Unit 4

Short vowel sounds

1 **Listen.** Notice the pronunciation of the underlined vowels. 🎧**142**

a	e	i	o	u
c<u>a</u>mera	r<u>e</u>d	h<u>i</u>m	h<u>o</u>t	l<u>u</u>nch

In English, we have short vowel sounds and long vowel sounds.

The vowel sound is usually short when there is a single vowel with a consonant before and one or two consonants after the vowel.

2 **Listen and repeat.** Circle the word that *doesn't* have a short vowel sound. 🎧**143**

1. c<u>a</u>mel, m<u>a</u>n, (plane,) c<u>a</u>t, p<u>a</u>nda
2. l<u>e</u>sson, desk, chess, sell, teach
3. kid, pink, wild, it, <u>i</u>nsect
4. d<u>o</u>lphin, food, stop, dog, f<u>o</u>rest
5. h<u>u</u>sband, f<u>u</u>nny, much, buy, cup

3 **Work in pairs.** Look at pages 84–85. Find at least one word for each short vowel sound and write it in the correct column.

a	e	i	o	u

Irregular Verbs

Infinitive	Past simple	Past participle	Infinitive	Past simple	Past participle
be	were	been	lead	led	led
beat	beat	beaten	leave	left	left
become	became	become	lend	lent	lent
begin	began	begun	let	let	let
bend	bent	bent	light	lit	lit
bite	bit	bitten	lose	lost	lost
bleed	bled	bled	make	made	made
blow	blew	blown	mean	meant	meant
break	broke	broken	meet	met	met
bring	brought	brought	pay	paid	paid
build	built	built	put	put	put
burn	burnt	burnt	quit	quit	quit
buy	bought	bought	read	read	read
carry	carried	carried	rise	rose	risen
catch	caught	caught	run	ran	run
choose	chose	chosen	say	said	said
come	came	come	see	saw	seen
cost	cost	cost	sell	sold	sold
cut	cut	cut	send	sent	sent
deal	dealt	dealt	set	set	set
dig	dug	dug	sew	sewed	sewn
do	did	done	shake	shook	shaken
draw	drew	drawn	shine	shone	shone
drink	drank	drunk	show	showed	shown
drive	drove	driven	shut	shut	shut
dry	dried	dried	sing	sang	sung
eat	ate	eaten	sink	sank	sunk
fall	fell	fallen	sit	sat	sat
feed	fed	fed	sleep	slept	slept
feel	felt	felt	slide	slid	slid
fight	fought	fought	speak	spoke	spoken
find	found	found	spend	spent	spent
fly	flew	flown	spin	spun	spun
forget	forgot	forgotten	stand	stood	stood
forgive	forgave	forgiven	steal	stole	stolen
freeze	froze	frozen	stick	stuck	stuck
fry	fried	fried	sting	stung	stung
get	got	got	sweep	swept	swept
give	gave	given	swim	swam	swum
go	went	gone	swing	swung	swung
grow	grew	grown	take	took	taken
hang	hung	hung	teach	taught	taught
have	had	had	tear	tore	torn
hear	heard	heard	tell	told	told
hide	hid	hidden	think	thought	thought
hit	hit	hit	throw	threw	thrown
hold	held	held	understand	understood	understood
hurt	hurt	hurt	wake	woke	woken
keep	kept	kept	wear	wore	worn
knit	knitted	knitted	win	won	won
know	knew	known	write	wrote	written

Greetings: Formal and informal

1 **Listen and read.** 🎧 **156**

Formal

          Linh: Hello, Mrs Tran. How are you?

Mrs Tran: Very well, thank you. And you, Linh?

Greeting	Responding
• Hello (Mrs Tran). How are you? • Good morning / afternoon / evening. How are you?	• Very well, thank you. And you? • Fine, thank you. How are you?

2 **Listen and read.** 🎧 **157**

Informal

      Linh: Hi, Thao. How are you doing?

Thao: I'm OK, thanks. How are you?

Greeting	Responding
• Hi! How are you? • Hello. How's it going? • Hi. How are you doing?	• I'm OK, thanks. • Hi. I'm fine, thanks. How are you? • Great, thanks. How about you? • Not bad, thanks. You?

Introductions: Formal and informal

3 **Listen and read.** 🎧 **158**

Formal

Linh: Mrs Tran, I'd like to introduce you to Mai.

Mrs Tran: Hello, Mai. It's a pleasure to meet you.

Making an introduction	Responding
• I'd like to introduce you to Mai. • I'd like you to meet Mai.	• It's a pleasure to meet you, Mai. • I'm very pleased to meet you.

4 **Listen and read.** 🎧 **159**

Informal

Thao: Hi. My name's Thao. Nice to meet you.

Linh: Hi, Thao. I'm Linh. Very nice to meet you, too.

Making an introduction	Responding
• Hi. I'm Thao. • Hi there. My name's Thao. Nice to meet you. • Hi, Thao. This is Linh. She's in my class. • This is Linh. She's a student at my school.	• Hi, Thao. My name's Linh. Nice to meet you. • Hello. I'm Linh. Very nice to meet you, too. • Hi, Linh. Nice to meet you. • Hi, Linh. I'm Thao. It's nice to meet you.

Expressing thanks: Formal and informal

5 **Listen and read.** 🎧160

Formal

Mr Silva: You've been very helpful. That's very kind of you.

Lara: It's my pleasure.

Expressing thanks	Responding
• Thank you. That's very kind of you. • Thank you. That's very thoughtful. • I'm very grateful.	• It's my pleasure. • Don't mention it. • It's no trouble at all.

6 **Listen and read.** 🎧161

Informal

Lara: Wow! That's so nice of you. Thanks a lot.

Victor: You're welcome.

Expressing thanks	Responding
• Thanks. • Thanks a lot. • Thanks very much.	• You're welcome. • No problem. • Any time.

Taking turns

7 **Listen and read.** 🎧162

Ana: We have to practise the dialogue on page 27. Who should go first?

Lara: Why don't you?

Ana: OK, sure.

Asking	Responding	Agreeing
• Who should go first? • Do you want to say the first line? • Who would like to start?	• Why don't you? • I went first the last time. • I'd like to. • Is it OK if I go first?	• OK, sure. • All right. • Of course.

Asking for and giving information

8 **Listen and read.** 🎧 163

Victor:	Hi, Ana. Can you tell me what the maths homework is?
Ana:	I think we just need to study for the test.
Victor:	I wonder what the test is on ... Do you have any idea?
Ana:	I'm not sure, but I think it's on all of Unit 3.

Asking for information	Responding
• Can you tell me ...? • I'd like to know ... • I wonder ... • Do you have any idea?	• I think ... • As far as I know, ... • I'm not sure, but I think ... • I don't know, sorry.

Giving a presentation

9 **Listen and read.** 🎧 164

Lara:	Today, we're going to learn about endangered animals.
Victor:	We'll start by describing different endangered animals.
Lara:	Have a look at this poster. You'll see that there are a lot of endangered animals in the world.
Victor:	Next, let's look at where they come from.
Lara:	As you can see, there's a lot to learn! Any questions?

Beginning	Middle	End
• Today, we're going to ... • Today, I'm going to ... • We'll / I'll start by ...	• Have a look at ... • You'll see that ... • Next, let's look at ...	• As you can see, ... • Any questions?

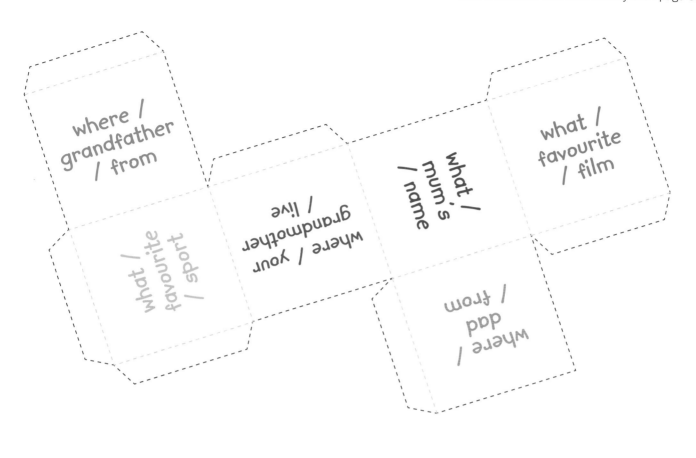

where / grandfather / from

what / favourite / sport

where / your grandmother / live

what / mum's / name

where / dad / from

what / favourite / film

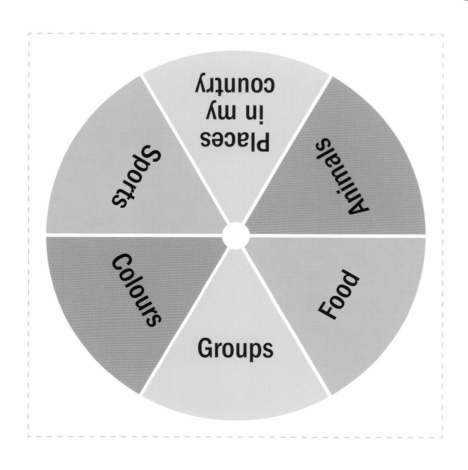

Places in my country

Sports

Animals

Colours

Food

Groups

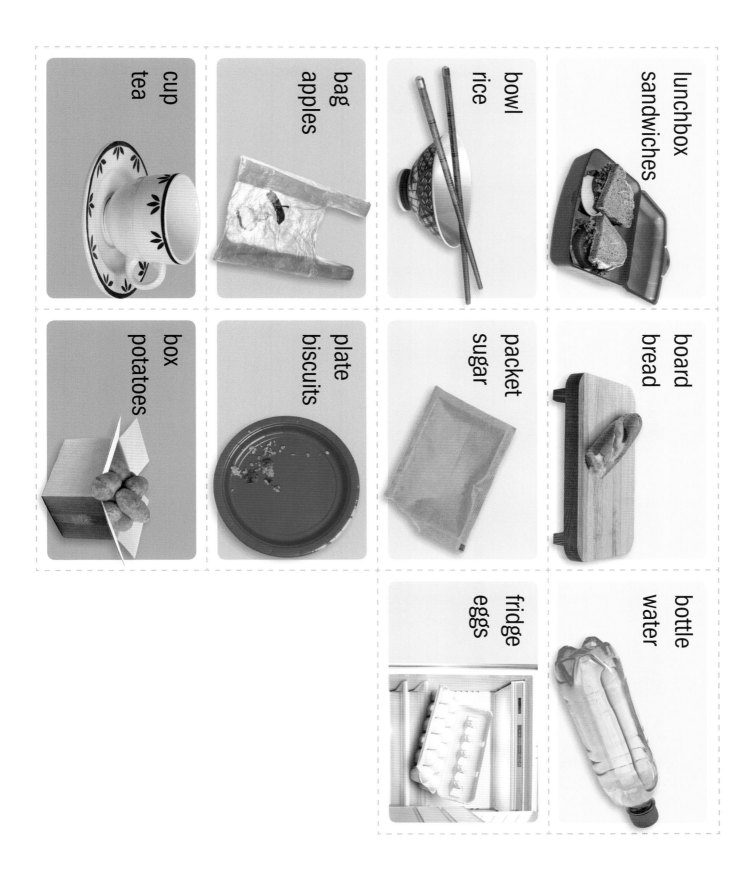

cup
tea

bag
apples

bowl
rice

lunchbox
sandwiches

box
potatoes

plate
biscuits

packet
sugar

board
bread

fridge
eggs

bottle
water

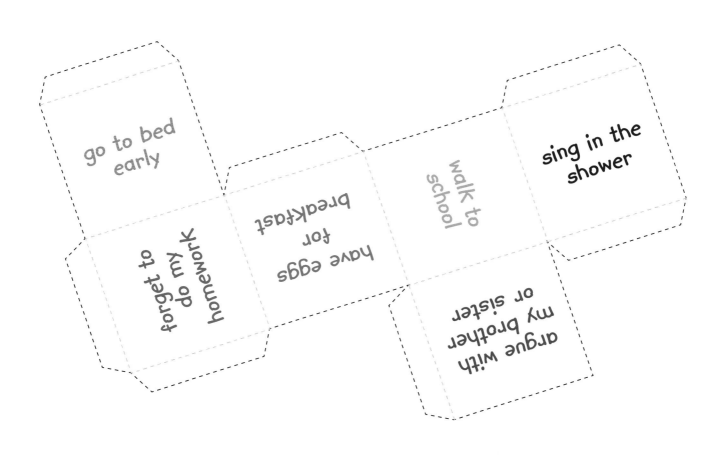

go to bed early

sing in the shower

forget to do my homework

have eggs for breakfast

walk to school

argue with my brother or sister

Tech-o-ball looks like a ball, but you can control it with your phone and play a lot of games with it.

Helidrone flies around your home. It can take photos and videos.

The SuperClock is a robot alarm clock. It jumps onto the floor and hides!

HandyReach helps people who can't move their arms. It can pick up things.

SpaceDroid is an astronaut robot. It helps astronauts on the International Space Station.

Roboclean cleans your floor.

Make it Basic is a robot kit. You build the robot and you decide what it can do.

DogBot is a robot dog. It can understand voice commands.

I want to be a computer scientist.

I want to buy a robot dog.

I don't understand my maths homework.

I want to build a robot.

I want to study engineering at university.

I want to design computer games.

Foping Nature Reserve

- Where: China
- Size: 350 square kilometres
- Number of pandas: 80–100
- Other animals: leopards, golden monkeys and black bears

Ranthambore National Park

- Where: India
- Size: 392 square kilometres
- Number of tigers: 22
- Other animals: hyenas, wild boar and leopards

Yala National Park

- Where: Sri Lanka
- Size: 979 square kilometres
- Number of elephants: 350
- Other animals: leopards, bears and buffalo

Sepilok Orangutan Sanctuary

- Where: Borneo
- Size: 43 square kilometres
- Number of orangutans: 60–80
- Other animals: sun bears, gibbons and pygmy elephants

Ngamba Island Chimpanzee Sanctuary

- Where: Uganda
- Size: ½ square kilometre
- Number of chimpanzees: 49
- Other animals: wild birds and fish

National Bison Range

- Where: USA
- Size: 74 square kilometres
- Number of bison: 350
- Other animals: bears, antelope and deer

Foping Nature Reserve

Ranthambore National Park

Yala National Park

Sepilok Orangutan Sanctuary

Ngamba Island Chimpanzee Sanctuary

National Bison Range

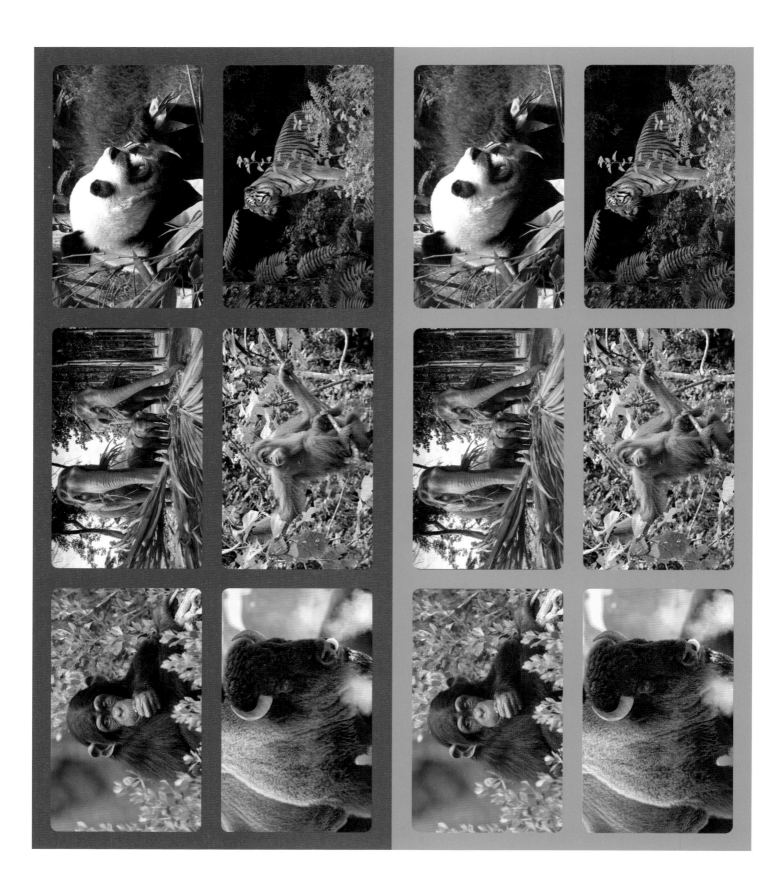

impact
WORKBOOK
FOUNDATION A

SERIES EDITORS
JoAnn (Jodi) Crandall
Joan Kang Shin

Unit 0	Welcome!	2
Unit 1	Family Matters	16
Unit 2	A Different Education	26
	Units 1–2 Review	36
Unit 3	Robots and Us	38
Unit 4	Part of Nature	48
	Units 3–4 Review	58
	You Decide Activities	104

NATIONAL GEOGRAPHIC
L E A R N I N G

Australia · Brazil · Mexico · Singapore · United Kingdom · United States

Unit 0
Welcome!

THE ALPHABET

1 Write the missing letters.

A a ___ ___   C ___ ___ ___ ___ ___ ___ f G ___ ___ ___ ___ i ___ ___ ___ ___

L ___ ___ m ___ ___ ___ ___ ___ p ___ ___ ___ ___ S ___ ___ ___ ___ u

___ ___   W ___ ___ ___ ___ y ___ ___

2 Write the words in alphabetical order. Then spell them out loud.

| class | pencil | paper | name | ~~book~~ | homework |

1. _____book_____   4. _____

2. _____   5. _____

3. _____   6. _____

3 Listen. Write the cities you hear. Use a map to find the country for each city. Write, say and spell each country name. Then check your answers with a partner. 🎧 002

Example: _____Athens_____   _____Greece_____

1. _____   _____

2. _____   _____

3. _____   _____

4. _____   _____

5. _____   _____

6. _____   _____

7. _____   _____

8. _____   _____

GREETINGS AND INTRODUCTIONS

1 **Read and match.** Write the letter on the line.

___d___ 1. Hello!

_____ 2. What's your name?

_____ 3. Where are you from?

_____ 4. Lara, this is my teacher, Mr Patel.

a. Nice to meet you!

b. I'm from Singapore.

c. My name is Raina.

d. Hi!

2 **Read.** Complete the conversation.

Mrs Lee: Hello! My (1) _____ is Mrs Lee. What's your (2) _____?

Jian: (3) _____ name's Jian. Nice to (4) _____ you, Mrs Lee.

Mrs Lee: Hi, Jian! Good to meet (5) _____, too!

Jian: (6) _____ are you from?

Mrs Lee: I'm (7) _____ Shanghai.

Jian: Oh, really? (8) This _____ Peter. He's from Shanghai, too.

Mrs Lee: (9) _____, Peter.

Peter: Hello, Mrs Lee. (10) _____ to meet you!

3 **Listen.** Write a response using answers about yourself. 🎧003

1. _____

2. _____

3. _____

4. _____

GRAMMAR

Subject pronouns and *be*

Full forms	Contractions
I am from Buenos Aires. **It is** in Argentina.	**I'm** from Buenos Aires. **It's** in Argentina.
Juan **is** from Mexico City. **He is** Mexican.	**You're** from Mexico. **He's** Mexican too.
We are not from England.	**We're** not / We **aren't** from England.
Paula's family **is** Canadian. **She is** from Toronto.	**They're** Canadian. **She's** from Toronto.

1 **Read.** Write the full form of *be*.

1. you _____are_____

2. I _____

3. he /she _____

4. they _____

5. it _____

6. we _____

2 **Write the contractions.** Use the words from Activity 1.

1. _____you're_____

2. _____

3. _____

4. _____

5. _____

6. _____

3 **Read and write.** Use a map if necessary.

1. Berta is from Santiago. _____She isn't_____ Australian.

2. Kyle is from London. _____ French.

3. Lucas is from Rio de Janeiro. _____ Brazilian.

4. Valerie and Christine are from Chicago. _____ American.

5. Mei and I are from Shanghai. _____ Malaysian.

6. You're from Costa Rica. _____ Argentinian.

4 **Write three sentences.** Say where you and two other people are from.

1. _____

2. _____

3. _____

4

CLASSROOM LANGUAGE

1 **Read.** Who do you think is speaking? Write **T** for *Teacher* or **S** for *Student*.

1. 'Be quiet, please!' _____T_____

2. 'I'm sorry I'm late, Mrs Reed.' _____

3. 'Open your books at page 23.' _____

4. 'Listen to the recording.' _____

5. 'Excuse me, how do you spell "welcome"?' _____

6. 'Can you repeat that, please?' _____

7. 'Work in pairs.' _____

8. 'Mrs Reed, what does "nationality" mean?' _____

2 **Read.** Complete the conversation with the phrases from the box.

| How do you spell   Open your books   Sit down   sorry I'm late   What page is it   work in pairs |

Mr Jansen: (1) _____ , please. Today, let's learn about cities and

countries. (2) _____ at page 110.

Thomas: Hello. I'm (3) _____ , Mr Jansen.

Mr Jansen: Hurry up please, Thomas! Sit down and open your book.

Thomas: (4) _____ , please?

Mr Jansen: It's page 110, Thomas. OK, let's start. Look at the photograph. Who knows
which city that is? Yes, Juliana?

Juliana: It's Moscow.

Mr Jansen: That's right! (5) _____ 'Moscow', Juliana?

Juliana: M-O-S-C-O-W.

Mr Jansen: That's right. Now (6) _____ . Do Activity 1 with
your partner.

MONTHS OF THE YEAR AND DAYS OF THE WEEK

1 **Find and circle ten words in the puzzle.** Then write them in the correct box.

E	B	J	A	N	U	A	R	Y	F	C	A	Y
F	H	I	M	O	E	W	U	D	Y	S	R	M
E	P	L	I	V	T	D	A	G	R	S	A	S
B	R	A	X	E	E	H	D	E	U	Y	J	A
R	R	Q	C	M	N	A	U	B	I	S	D	T
U	D	A	S	B	T	J	G	R	O	L	T	U
A	D	T	C	E	L	U	R	O	S	F	K	R
R	L	A	P	R	I	L	T	E	B	D	E	D
Y	M	O	N	D	A	Y	H	S	W	D	A	A
E	T	Y	P	W	E	D	N	E	S	D	A	Y
D	E	T	N	D	A	B	P	W	O	A	R	R

Months

April

Days

2 **Write.** Complete the tables from Activity 1 with the remaining months and days.

3 **Listen.** Write the month of each person's birthday. ∩ 004

1. Nadia _____   3. Salma _____

2. John _____   4. Rashi _____

SEASONS

1 **Look and draw.** Draw a picture to show each season.

spring	fall
summer	winter

NUMBERS

1 **Write the numbers.**

1. _____ thirty-five

2. _____ one hundred and twenty

3. _____ six hundred and eighty-two

4. _____ one thousand nine hundred and fifty-seven

5. 396 _____

6. 983 _____

2 **Listen.** Complete the sentences. 🎧 005

1. It's the _____ race of the day.

2. Emilia finishes _____ .

3. Paula is _____ .

4. Sara is _____ .

5. Roberto is _____ .

6. Miguel is _____ .

3 **Write about your next birthday.** Include the month, day and season. Use a calendar.

_____

_____

COLOURS

1 **Read.** Tick ✓ the correct sentences. Rewrite the incorrect sentences.

☐   1. Elephants are red. _____

☐   2. Zebras are black and white. _____

☐   3. Apples are blue. _____

☐   4. Chocolate is brown. _____

☐   5. The sun is purple. _____

☐   6. Rice is usually white or brown. _____

2 **Read and write.** Use the clues to complete the puzzle with the colours.

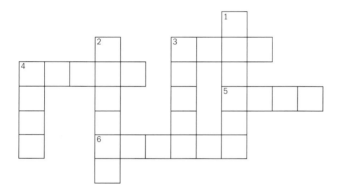

Across

3. the colour of the sea
4. yellow + blue
5. red + white
6. yellow + red

Down

1. red + blue
2. the colour of a banana
3. the colour of a teddy bear
4. black + white

TELLING THE TIME

1 **Listen.** Circle the clock with the time you hear. 🎧006

1. `5.00` `6.00`
2. `3.30` `3.00`
3. `5.15` `5.00`
4. `7.45` `8.00`
5. `12.30` `12.15`
6. `2.45` `1.45`

2 **Write.** Complete the sentences with your own information.

1. I have breakfast at _half past seven_ .

2. I go to school at _____ .

3. I have lunch at _____ .

4. I watch TV at _____ .

5. I go to bed at _____ .

3 **Read and look.** Say and write what time it is. Use *in the morning/afternoon/evening*.

`4.30`   `7.00`  `11.15`  `8.45`  `5.45`

1. Edgar is eating breakfast. What time is it? _____

   _____

2. Julian is in a maths class. What time is it? _____

   _____

3. Susannah is playing football. What time is it? _____

   _____

4. Mary is playing video games. What time is it? _____

   _____

5. Felipe is going to bed. What time is it? _____

   _____

GRAMMAR

Object pronouns

Come with **me**.	The food is bad. Don't eat **it**.
This book is for **you**.	Please give the ball to **us**.
I really like **him**.	I can share my lunch with **you**.
Can you go with **her?**	Let's help **them**.

1 **Read.** Underline six object pronouns in the paragraph.

I like apples. They're good for you. Do you like them? My mother buys apples for us at the market. She always cuts an apple for my baby brother. She gives him one piece at a time. He can't eat it all – it's too big! So, my mum gives the rest to me.

2 **Read.** Complete each sentence with a word from the box.

her	him	it	me	them	us	you

1. Dad is thirsty. Please take this glass of water to _____ .

2. Maria is very nice. Do you know _____ ?

3. I want to watch TV. Can you watch with _____ ?

4. You look sad. How can I help _____ ?

5. Let's go to the park. We can take the dog with _____ .

6. I need the computer. I'll turn _____ on.

7. The boys want to see the new car. Let's show it to _____ .

3 **Rewrite each sentence.** Replace the underlined word(s) with an object pronoun.

1. Share your pens with <u>Leila and Teresa</u>. *Share your pens with them.* _____

2. Open <u>your book</u> at page 130. _____

3. I visit <u>Charles</u> at four o'clock. _____

4. The pencils belong to <u>Marta</u>. _____

5. Dad is making a cake for <u>you and me</u>. _____

GRAMMAR

Possessive adjectives

my house	**his** toys	**its** colours	**your** books
your cat	**her** pencil	**our** food	**their** bus
Questions			
Is it her **bag**? Is it **your** book?			

1 **Read.** Complete the sentences with the correct word.

1. The bag belongs to me. It's _____my_____ bag.

2. The students have got green books. _____ books are on the table.

3. The blue shoes belong to Sara. They're _____ shoes.

4. 'This is _____ school,' say Liz and Ivy.

5. The water bottle is Erik's. It's _____ bottle.

6. The bird is asleep. It's in _____ nest.

GRAMMAR

Possessive pronouns

my house	→	The house is **mine**.	**our** food	→	The food is **ours**.
your cat	→	The cat is **yours**.	**your** books	→	The books are **yours**.
his toys	→	The toys are **his**.	**their** bus	→	The bus is **theirs**.
her pencil	→	The pencil is **hers**.			
Question					
Whose car is this? It's **ours**.					

1 **Write.** Complete the sentences with the correct word.

1. My book is not yellow. The red one is _____mine_____ .

2. Glenda doesn't eat sweets. Those chocolates aren't _____ .

3. We've got a new car. The blue one over there is _____ .

4. '_____ bicycle is that? David, is it _____ ?'

5. Victor took Julie's keys. He doesn't know where _____ are.

PLURALS

1 **Read.** Decide if the word is singular, plural, or both. Tick ✓ the correct box. If the word is singular, write the plural. If the word is plural, write the singular.

	1	2 or more			1	2 or more	
1. child	✓	☐	*children*	5. feet	☐	☐	_____
2. babies	☐	☐	_____	6. mouse	☐	☐	_____
3. tomato	☐	☐	_____	7. quiz	☐	☐	_____
4. sheep	☐	☐	_____	8. women	☐	☐	_____

GRAMMAR

Definite and indefinite articles

The book is on **the** desk.
There's **a** mouse in the classroom! **The** mouse is running.
I don't want **an** animal in the classroom. **The** students don't like mice.

---

1 **Read and circle the correct word.**

1. **A / The** people at my school are very nice.

2. Is there **a / an** animal at the window?

3. **A / The** men at the club know my father.

4. Maths is **a / an** difficult subject for me.

5. **An / The** teacher is Mrs Maddox.

6. I need **a / an** green apple for the pie.

2 **Read.** Complete the sentences with *a, an* or *the.*

1. There's _____ bakery near my home. _____ bakers there make delicious bread.

2. Do you have _____ egg? I want to make _____ cake.

3. _____ computer on _____ desk belongs to my mother.

4. A: What's in _____ box? It's very heavy!
   B: New books for _____ science students.

5. She's eating _____ orange. It's from _____ tree in our garden.

6. _____ students are happy today. _____ teacher didn't give them any homework.

GRAMMAR

Demonstrative adjectives

This book is very interesting.
I love **that** dress over there. It's really colourful!
Do you want some of **these** oranges? They're delicious.
We don't know **those** students! Maybe they're new.

1 **Listen and colour.** 🎧 **007**

1.

3.

2.

4.

2 **Read.** Complete each sentence with *this*, *that*, *these* or *those*.

1. The books on that table belong to Lee. _____ pencils are his, too.

2. Today is my birthday. I'm 11 _____ year.

3. Look at _____ cat. She always sits here on my keyboard.

4. Where can we put _____ flowers? We can't keep them here.

5. Look over there! I don't know who _____ car belongs to.

3 **Write.** Describe three things in your home. Use *this*, *that*, *these* and *those*.

1. This is my desk. _____

2. _____

3. _____

4. _____

GRAMMAR

Prepositions of place

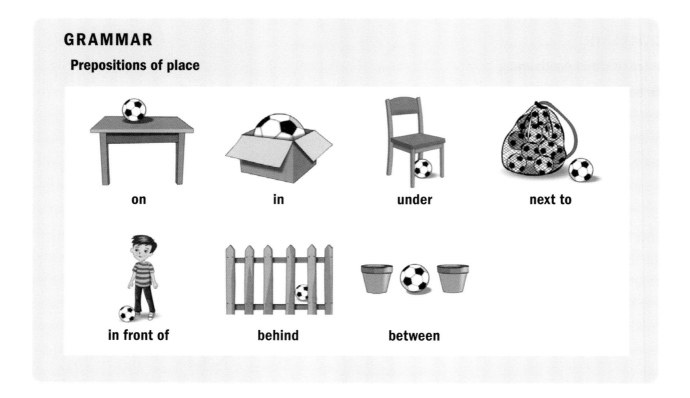

on

in

under

next to

in front of

behind

between

1 **Read.** Circle the best word to complete each sentence.

1. The children are **in front of / behind** the sofa. I can't see them.

2. My pencil is on the floor, **under / on** my desk.

3. There's a little green car **between / in** those two buses.

4. Please come and stand **in front of / under** the class.

5. The market is on this street, **in / next to** the school.

6. She put her books **in / behind** her bag to take them home.

7. The pens **on / between** the desk belong to Greta.

2 **Listen and draw.** Then compare your answers with a partner. Say where the items are. 🎧008

1.	2.	3.

GRAMMAR

Countable and uncountable nouns

Countable nouns	Uncountable nouns
an egg → **three** egg**s**	juice → **some** juice
a book → **some** book**s**	bread → **some** bread

1 **Organise.** Write the words in the correct column.

apple	biscuit	bread	cheese	egg	juice	milk	pasta	rice	strawberry

Countable	Uncountable

2 **Listen.** Complete the shopping list with the words you hear. 🎧 009

some _bread_

_____ apples

milk

_____ eggs

six _____

chicken

rice

3 **Write.** You're going food shopping. Write five things you need. Use *a*, *an*, *some* or a number for each item.

some orange juice

_____

_____

_____

Unit 1
Family Matters

1 **Look at the family tree.** Complete each sentence with a word from the box.

| children | died | ~~four~~ | generations | grandfather | husband | is married to | son | wife |

1. Robert and Ida have got _____ four _____ granddaughters.

2. Paul and Elaine have got three _____ .

3. David is Serena and Tony's _____ .

4. Elaine _____ Paul.

5. Ida _____ in 2014.

6. Sally is Thomas's _____ .

7. Serena's _____ is called Tony.

8. There are four _____ in the family.

16

2 **Listen.** Tick the questions you hear. 🎧 **010**

1. a. What's your favourite food? ☐
   b. What's your favourite sport? ☑

2. a. What's your husband's name? ☐
   b. What's your son's name? ☐

3. a. Where are your parents from? ☐
   b. Where are your grandparents from? ☐

4. a. What's his name? ☐
   b. What's her name? ☐

3 **Listen.** Write the number of the sentence that goes with each photo. 🎧 **011**

a.

b.

c.

d. ①

e.

f.

4 **Listen to the questions.** Write answers. 🎧 **012**

1. _____

2. _____

3. _____

GRAMMAR

Be and *have got*

Be	Have got	
I**'m** an explorer.	I**'ve got** two sisters.	**am** = **'m**
You **aren't** an explorer.	You**'ve got** one brother.	**is** = **'s**
Is he a photographer?	He **hasn't got** famous grandparents.	**are** = **'re**
We**'re** explorers.	We**'ve got** similar interests.	**have** = **'ve**
Are they good at singing?	**Have** they **got** any children?	**has** = **'s**

You can use the verb **be** with nouns (*I**'m** an explorer.*) and adjectives (*It**'s** dangerous.*)

To form the negative, use *not* or add *n't*: *I**'m not** an explorer. / We **aren't** happy.*

To ask a question, change the word order: ***Are** you an explorer?*

We use **have got** to talk about things that are ours (*I**'ve got** two sisters.*) or to describe people (*She**'s got** long hair.*).

To form the negative, use *not* or add *n't They **have not got**/**haven't got** their tickets.*

To ask a question, change the word order: ***Has** he **got** blue eyes?*

1 Circle the correct words.

1. I**'m not** / **aren't** a photographer.

2. She**'s got** / **'ve got** two cats.

3. **Are** / **Is** they explorers?

4. They**'ve got** / **'s got** one daughter.

2 Read and match the two parts of the sentence. Write the letter on the line.

_C_ 1. Alexandra Cousteau has got

_____ 2. Jennifer is

_____ 3. Richard and Meave Leakey are

_____ 4. Is your sister good at

_____ 5. I'm interested in volcanoes,

_____ 6. Have you got

a. but my friend isn't.

b. sport?

c. a famous grandfather.

d. any pets?

e. Conrad Anker's wife.

f. Louise and Samira's parents.

3 Now listen and check your answers. 🎧 **013**

4 Complete the sentences using the correct form of the words.

1. The book _____ is _____ (be / ✓) really good.

2. Johann _____ (have got / ✗) any sisters.

3. Some of the insects in the rain forest _____ (be / ✓) dangerous.

4. The children _____ (be / ✗) tall enough to ride the rollercoaster.

5. We _____ (have got / ✓) new ice skates.

6. Mrs Moreau _____ (be / ✓) French.

5 Listen to the boy. Write the words he uses to describe each family member. 🎧 014

This is my dad. He (1) _____ an architect. He (2) _____ two older brothers. He (3) _____ really (4) _____ and (5) _____ .

This is my mum. She (6) _____ a photographer. She (7) _____ a really nice camera. My mum's (8) _____ at cooking too, and she makes delicious cakes.

Ben (9) _____ my brother. He's (10) _____ in films and he's (11) _____ at acting. He often plays with me. I'm glad I haven't got a (12) _____ brother!

Jane is my sister. She (13) _____ three years old. She's very (14) _____ . She (15) _____ a new drum kit and it's very (16) _____ !

6 Write sentences about two people in your family or a famous family. Use *be* and *have got* and words from the box.

| annoying | friendly | funny | mean | noisy | rude |

_____

_____

_____

Omelettes!
How do you eat yours?

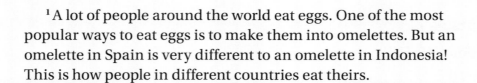

[1] A lot of people around the world eat eggs. One of the most popular ways to eat eggs is to make them into omelettes. But an omelette in Spain is very different to an omelette in Indonesia! This is how people in different countries eat theirs.

[2] Rudi has got two brothers and one sister. They live in Jambi in Indonesia. Their favourite breakfast is *telur dadar* – an Indonesian omelette. Their grandmother makes it for them every morning. She uses ten eggs each day! The omelettes have got garlic, onions and chilli in them. They're delicious!

[3] Akira lives with her mum and dad in Tokyo. Her favourite snack is her mum's *tamagoyaki*. It's a thin Japanese omelette. Akira eats this five times a week. Her mum adds two teaspoons of sugar and one teaspoon of soy sauce to the eggs. She then cooks the eggs in a hot pan. It's really tasty!

[4] Maria's grandmother makes *tortilla de patatas* for her family at least four times a week. She uses six eggs, three large potatoes and one large onion. Maria loves her grandmother's omelettes.

2 **Look at the numbers in the article.** Circle the correct answer.

Paragraph number	Number in the article	Answer
2	two	(a.) number of brothers Rudi has got b. number of sisters Rudi has got
2	ten	a. how many omelettes Rudi's grandmother makes b. how many eggs Rudi's grandmother uses
3	two	a. teaspoons of sugar b. teaspoons of soy sauce
3	five	a. number of times Akira eats a snack each week b. number of times Akira eats *tamagoyaki* each week
4	six	a. number of potatoes b. number of eggs

3 **Look at the table of ingredients.** Read *Omelettes! How do you eat yours?* again. Tick the boxes if the person uses that ingredient.

	Rudi's grandmother	Akira's mum	Maria's grandmother
Eggs	✓		
Onions	✓		
Potatoes			
Sugar			
Soy sauce			
Garlic			
Chilli			

4 **Write about your favourite snack.** Who makes it for you? What ingredients are in it? How often do you eat it?

_____

_____

_____

_____

GRAMMAR

Countable and uncountable nouns

Countable nouns	Uncountable nouns
There are six eggs in this omelette.	**There's some** honey in the cupboard.
Are there any peppers?	**Is there any** coffee?
Yes, there are. **There are some** peppers, but **there aren't any** onions.	No, there isn't. **There isn't any** coffee, but **there's some** tea.

If we can count something, it's a countable noun: *eggs, peppers, onions*. We generally add an -s to make the plural. We can put *a/an* or a number before a countable noun: *an egg, six onions*.

If you can't count something, it's an uncountable noun: *bread, milk, water*. These words don't have a plural form.

1 **Look at Mari's shopping list.** Listen and write the numbers you hear in the boxes. If you don't hear a number, leave it blank. 🎧 016

6	onions	C
☐	tomatoes	___
☐	garlic	___
☐	beefburgers	___
☐	rice	___
☐	coffee	___
☐	bread	___
☐	eggs	___

2 **Look at Mari's shopping list again.** Write **C** for *countable* and **U** for *uncountable* next to each word.

3 **Read the conversation between Polly and her grandmother.** Complete the sentences with words from the box. You can use a word more than once.

| any | are | is | some | there |

Polly: Grandma, how do you make your apple cake?

Grandma: First, we need (1) _____ apples. How many apples (2) _____ there?

Polly: (3) _____ are six apples in the fruit bowl. How many do we need?

Grandma: Only four, so that's fine. We also need (4) _____ flour. That's in the cupboard, here. Is there (5) _____ butter in the fridge?

Polly: I'll look ... yes, there's some butter.

Grandma: And we need brown sugar. (6) _____ there (7) _____ brown sugar in the cupboard?

Polly: And we mustn't forget the spices. What do we need?

Grandma: Polly, there aren't (8) _____ spices in my apple cake.

4 **Answer the questions.**

1. Are there any eggs in the kitchen? ✗ No, there aren't.

2. Is there a pineapple in the fruit bowl? ✓ _____

3. Is there any milk in the fridge? ✓ _____

4. Are there any potatoes in the cupboard? ✗ _____

5 **Write questions.** Then look at the shelf and answer the questions.

1. there / any / tomato? Are there any tomatoes? → Yes, there are.

2. there / any / biscuit? _____ → _____

3. there / any / milk? _____ → _____

4. there / any / rice? _____ → _____

5. there / any / potato? _____ → _____

WRITING

When we want to connect pieces of information in a sentence, we use words such as *and* and *but*.
Use *and* to join similar pieces of information.
My brother is crazy about sport, **and** *he really likes to play music, too.*
Use *but* to contrast two different pieces of information.
My mum is very friendly, **but** *she's quite quiet.*

1 **Organise.**

1. Describe a member of your family. Look at the list of topics. Write two sentences about each topic. Is the information in the two sentences similar or different?

Appearance:	1	
	2	
Personality:	1	
	2	
Interests:	1	
	2	
Favourite food:	1	
	2	
Other information:	1	
	2	

2. Plan your writing. Look at the information in the table above. If the information is similar, join the sentences with *and*. If it is different, join the sentences with *but*.

Appearance:	1	She's got blue eyes.	My grandmother has got blue eyes and short grey hair.
	2	She's got short grey hair.	
Interests:	1	She likes music.	She likes music, but she doesn't play music now.
	2	She doesn't play music now.	

2 **Write.**

1. Go to page 39 in your Student's Book. Re-read the model.

2. Write your first draft. Check for organisation, content, punctuation, capitalisation and spelling.

3. Write your final draft. Share it with your teacher and classmates.

Now I can ...

· **talk about people in a family.**

Write two sentences about someone in your family.

_____

_____

☐ Yes, I can!
☐ I think I can.
☐ I need more practice.

Write two sentences about someone from a famous family.

_____

_____

· **use *be* and *have got* to talk about members of my family.**

Complete the sentences about your family.

I've got _____

He's _____

They're _____

She hasn't got _____

☐ Yes, I can!
☐ I think I can.
☐ I need more practice.

· **use countable and uncountable nouns.**

Write three sentences using these words.

| juice | parents | water |

_____

_____

_____

☐ Yes, I can!
☐ I think I can.
☐ I need more practice.

· **write about someone using the joining words *and* and *but*.**

Write four sentences about a friend. Join the sentences using *and* and *but*.

_____

_____

_____

_____

☐ Yes, I can!
☐ I think I can.
☐ I need more practice.

YOU DECIDE **Choose an activity.** Go to page 104.

Unit 2
A Different Education

1 **Read the clues.** Then complete the crossword.

Across

1. You can borrow books from a _____.
2. Our teacher gives us _____ for our work in class.
3. I do my _____ every night after school.
4. People speak different _____ in different countries.
5. You study different subjects in _____ during the school day.
6. We _____ speaking English so we get better.

Down

7. The other people in my class are my _____.
8. Televisions, tablets and computer monitors all have a _____.
9. A computer you can carry around is a _____.
10. I take photos with my _____.

L I B R A R Y

2 **Listen.** Read and tick **T** for *True* or **F** for *False*. Then rewrite any false sentences to make them true. 🎧 **017**

	T	F
1. The boy has got a new television.	☐	☐
2. The laptop hasn't got a camera.	☐	☐
3. The boy isn't very good at taking photos.	☐	☐
4. The teacher gives instructions for the students' homework in class.	☐	☐
5. Sixteen classmates have got a laptop.	☐	☐
6. There are 16 computers in the library.	☐	☐

_____

_____

3 **Read.** Complete the article with words from the box.

easy	difficult	different	instructions	language	practise	same

Some people think it's (1) _____ to learn a (2) _____
language. Other people think it's very (3) _____ and struggle for years.
Experts say that it's easier to learn another (4) _____ if you have a good
reason to learn it. Tomasz' mum is English. His dad is Polish. Tomasz was born in England.
His parents speak to him in English. Tomasz can't speak Polish, but he's got a lot of family in
Poland. Tomasz wants to learn Polish so he can speak to them. He likes to
(5) _____ Polish every day after school. His mum is also
learning Polish. Now, when they visit their family in Poland, they can all speak the
(6) _____ language!

4 **Answer the questions.**

1. Do you like learning a different language? What languages can you speak?

_____

2. What's your favourite subject?

_____

3. Which subjects are difficult?

_____

GRAMMAR

Present simple: Talking about routines, habits and permanent states

Affirmative	Negative
I **live** in Jakarta.	I **don't live** in Singapore.
You **learn** two languages in Year 4.	You **don't learn** Spanish until Year 5.
She **walks** to school every morning.	She **doesn't live** far from school.
Questions	
Do you **like** pasta?	
What does she **want** for dinner?	

To form the present simple: *I **live** in Jakarta. We **watch** TV.*
For he/she/it add *-s* or *-es*: *She live**s** in Jakarta. He watch**es** TV.*

To form the negative, use *don't* or *doesn't* and the infinitive without *to.*
*I **don't listen** to the radio. He **doesn't want** ice cream.*

To ask a question, use *do* or *does.* ***Do** you want breakfast?*
***Does** he travel by car?*

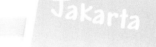

❶ Circle the correct word to complete the sentences.

1. Simon **like** / **(likes)** science and maths.

2. Miguel's grandparents **live** / **lives** in Quito.

3. My sister **teach** / **teaches** English in Beijing.

4. We **doesn't** / **don't** visit our friends every weekend.

5. The orchestra **practises** / **practise** five times a week.

❷ Read the questions and the answers. Listen and complete the questions. 🎧 **018**

1. _____Does_____ your brother _____play_____ football?   Yes, he does.

2. Where _____ your sister _____ ?   In Toronto.

3. _____ you _____ your grandparents after school?   Yes, I do.

4. What time _____ he _____ home?   At seven o'clock.

3 **Read the article.** Complete the text with the correct words. Then listen and check your answers. 🎧 **019**

> Claude is 11 years old. He (1) _____ (live) in South Africa with his parents. He's got two sisters, Eve and Tola. They're both six years old – they're twins. Claude (2) _____ (get up) at 6 a.m. He (3) _____ (make) breakfast to help his parents. He (4) _____ (finish) breakfast at 6.30. At seven o'clock, the children (5) _____ (walk) three km (1.86 mi) to school. They (6) _____ (go) to school at the weekend. On Saturdays, they (7) _____ (go) to the market with their parents. They (8) _____ (buy) meat and potatoes.

4 **Look at the table.** Read the sentences and complete with the names and the correct form of the verb.

	Monday	Tuesday	Wednesday	Thursday	Friday	Weekend
Jenna	cooking	tennis	tennis	cooking	Spanish	tennis
Sam	cooking	football	football	story writing	football	piano
Emily	piano	piano	piano	piano	piano	tennis
Harry	football	football	football	football	football	football

1. ____Harry____ ____plays____ (play) football every day.

2. _____ _____ (play) the piano on weekdays.

3. _____ _____ (write) stories once a week.

4. _____ and _____ _____ (play) tennis at the weekend.

5 **Think about your own routine.** Write sentences using words from the box.

at the weekend	every day	once a week	on weekdays	twice a week

1. _____

2. _____

3. _____

1 **Listen and read.** As you read, think about the author's main point.
Tick the correct sentence. 🎧 **020**

1. Parents think their children are safer with animals. ☐

2. A disability doesn't have to stop you doing things in life. ☐

3. It's very difficult to train a guide dog. ☐

A DIFFERENT PAIR OF EYES

Laura is 15 years old. She lives with her mum in Liverpool, in England. Laura is blind. She lost her eyesight when she was 11 years old. At the time, Laura remembers thinking, 'I can't see. How can I do anything? What activities can I do? I can't play tennis now and I can't go running.'

But now, Ginny lives with Laura. Laura explains, 'Ginny is a Labrador retriever, and she's my best friend. She helps me with my daily activities. If I can't find something, Ginny helps me look for it. Now, I walk to school without Mum because Ginny helps me cross roads safely. She helps me in the supermarket. We go out together every day. She gives me so much independence.'

Ginny is a wonderful partner for Laura. Her mum says, 'I don't worry as much when Laura goes out now. I know that Ginny is there by her side. We both feel safer with Ginny around.'

And what about Laura's activities? She laughs and explains, 'I know now that you can succeed at anything you want to. I do so much more now I'm blind. I play tennis more – at least four times a week – at a tennis club for blind players. I also run every day. I've made so many more friends. But Ginny is my favourite. By a long way!'

2 **Tick the ways that Ginny helps Laura.**

1. Ginny helps Laura find things. ☐

2. Ginny helps Laura cross busy roads. ☐

3. Ginny lets Laura know if there is danger. ☐

4. Ginny carries shopping. ☐

5. Ginny gives Laura independence. ☐

3 **Put the following sentences in the correct order.**

1. Laura walks to school with Ginny. ☐

2. Laura thinks she can't do the activities she likes. ☐

3. Laura plays tennis four times a week. ☐

4. Laura loses her eyesight. ☐ 1

5. Laura runs every day. ☐

6. Laura gets a guide dog called Ginny. ☐

4 **Read *A Different Pair of Eyes* and *Growth Mindset* on Student's Book page 51 again.**
Read the sentences below. Write + (positive) if the speaker has a positive attitude,
and write – (negative) if the speaker has a negative attitude.

1. I'm not good at maths. I don't understand it. ☐ –

2. I want to succeed, so I work hard every day. ☐

3. Of course I can do that! ☐

4. I want to learn Spanish, but it looks too difficult. ☐

5. I'm really bad at science. ☐

5 **Change the negative sentences in Activity 4 and make them positive.**
Use your own ideas.

I'm good at maths. It's my favourite subject.
_____

_____

GRAMMAR

Adverbs of frequency: Saying how often you do something

0% ————————————————→ 100%

never   rarely   sometimes   often   always

He **never** goes online.   I **often** do my homework in the library.
They **rarely** meet up on weekdays.   I **always** use my laptop after school.
We **sometimes** walk home together.

We use adverbs of frequency to say **how often** we do things.

1 **Look at the advice for staying safe online.** Listen and write the adverbs of frequency. 🎧 021

1. _____Always_____ think before you post anything online.

2. _____ share personal information with people you don't know.

3. Make sure you change your password _____.

4. I _____ just leave my phone in my room and go outside.

5. Apps are _____ free, so make sure you don't spend too much money on them.

6. _____ make sure your parents know what you're looking at online.

2 **Complete the sentences about how to stay safe online.** Use two different adverbs of frequency.

1. Think about what you write online, and _____ check your messages before you post them.

2. _____ make friends with strangers online.

32

3 Read. Complete the sentences with the correct adverb of frequency.

We asked three 'tweens' – people between the ages of 8 and 12 – from different countries how long they spend online.

Claude, from South Africa

I've got a computer, but I haven't got a smartphone. There are some computers at school. We sometimes use them, but we rarely look at things online. We don't often get a good Internet connection.

Marianna, from Poland

My parents look at their smartphones all the time. My mum often checks her emails at the table, and dad sometimes plays games. I haven't got a smartphone so I never spend any time on one.

Jun, from Japan

Every day, I check my smartphone to see if I have messages from my friends. At school, we often work on laptops or tablets. And I always do my homework online. We upload it three or four times a week for our teachers.

always	never	often	rarely	sometimes

1. Claude _____*sometimes*_____ uses a computer at school.

2. Claude _____ goes online in class.

3. Marianna's dad _____ plays games on his phone.

4. Marianna _____ uses a smartphone.

5. Jun _____ looks at his smartphone.

6. Jun _____ uploads his homework for his teachers.

4 Write three sentences about youself. Use a different adverb of frequency in each sentence.

1. _____

2. _____

3. _____

WRITING

When we write about someone's daily routine, we use sequencing words such as:

first   then   next   before   after

These words tell the reader the order of events.

1 **Organise.**

1. Describe a day in your life. Look at the different times of day below. Think about your own day and list what you do at each time in the 'Things I do' column.

	Things I do	When/How often I do these things
Early morning:		
Mid morning:		
Lunchtime:		
Early afternoon:		
Mid afternoon:		
Late afternoon:		
Early evening:		
Late evening:		
Bedtime:		

2. How often do you do these things? Every day? At weekends? On weekdays? Once a week? Complete the 'When/How often I do these things' column.

3. Plan your writing. Look at the information in the table above. Remember to use sequencing words and adverbs of frequency to write your description.

2 **Write.**

1. Go to page 55 in your Student's Book. Re-read the model text.

2. Write your first draft. Check for organisation, content, punctuation, capitalisation and spelling.

3. Write your final draft. Share it with your teacher and classmates.

Now I can ...

· **talk about different types of schools.**

☐ Yes, I can!
☐ I think I can.
☐ I need more practice.

Write a sentence about your school day.

_____

Write a sentence about something you like doing at school.

_____

· **use the present simple to talk about routines, habits and permanent states.**

☐ Yes, I can!
☐ I think I can.
☐ I need more practice.

Complete two positive sentences and one negative sentence using a word from the box.

eat	go	live

I _____

He _____

We _____

· **use adverbs of frequency to talk about how often I do things.**

☐ Yes, I can!
☐ I think I can.
☐ I need more practice.

Complete the sentences for you, using an adverb of frequency.

I _____ eat sushi.

I _____ go to the cinema at the weekend.

I _____ watch television after school.

· **write about daily routines using sequencing words.**

☐ Yes, I can!
☐ I think I can.
☐ I need more practice.

Put these events into order. Write 1–4 in the boxes.

1. Then, I have breakfast. ☐

2. First, I get up at seven o'clock. ☐

3. After school, I visit my grandmother. ☐

4. Next, I go to school. ☐

YOU DECIDE **Choose an activity.** Go to page 105.

Units 1–2 Review

1 **Read.** Choose the word that best completes the sentences.

1. Maria is the mother of Sonia's father. Sonia is Maria's ____ .
   a. children   (b.) granddaughter   c. wife

2. Isabel ____ Sebastian, but they are very different people.
   a. is married to   b. died   c. succeeds

3. Eva is my new ____ . We're doing our English homework together.
   a. classmate   b. daughter   c. generation

4. Brigitte speaks four ____ : English, Spanish, Mandarin and French.
   a. lessons   b. languages   c. instructions

5. I've got a lot of ____ to do today. I'll start with maths.
   a. libraries   b. breakfast   c. homework

6. Paul takes photos of his sons with his new ____ .
   a. screen   b. camera   c. lesson

2 **Listen.** Read and tick **T** for *True* or **F** for *False*. 🎧 **022**

	T	F
1. Jay is good at the guitar.	☐	☐
2. Simon hasn't got a laptop.	☐	☐
3. Lisa thinks her little brother is funny.	☐	☐
4. Paola often watches television on weekdays.	☐	☐
5. Juan plays football three times a week.	☐	☐
6. Mrs Lopez hasn't got any children.	☐	☐

3 **Read.** Decide which answer (**a**, **b** or **c**) best fits each gap.

Elena (1) _____ an archaeologist. She (2) _____ in Italy, but she (3) _____ goes to Morocco for work. She (4) _____ her job because she works with (5) _____ good people. They (6) _____ kind and friendly.

When Elena is in Morocco, she works in the field (7) _____. When she's in Italy, she (8) _____ in a school. Elena (9) _____ an easy job – it's a lot of work! But she hasn't got (10) _____ problems with it. Her work makes her very happy.

1.	a. am	b. is	c. are
2.	a. live	b. don't live	c. lives
3.	a. often	b. never	c. every day
4.	a. love	b. loves	c. doesn't love
5.	a. some	b. any	c. rarely
6.	a. am	b. 's	c. 're
7.	a. sometimes	b. every day	c. never
8.	a. teaches	b. teach	c. don't teach
9.	a. have got	b. hasn't got	c. has got
10.	a. some	b. any	c. always

4 **Write.** Use the words in the box to say how often you do each activity.

always	at the weekend	never	often	on weekdays	rarely	sometimes	(twice) a week

1. have lunch at home _I rarely have lunch at home._____

2. do homework _____

3. go to the library _____

4. make breakfast for my parents _____

5. have dinner at a restaurant _____

6. listen to my teacher's instructions _____

7. use a laptop _____

8. visit a family member _____

Unit 3
Robots and Us

1 **Look at the pictures.** Complete each sentence with words from the box.

controls	doctor	hold	mouse	movable	online	pain

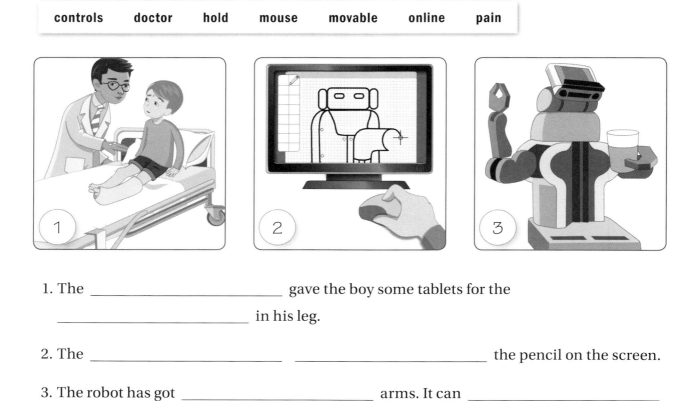

1. The _____ gave the boy some tablets for the
   _____ in his leg.

2. The _____ _____ the pencil on the screen.

3. The robot has got _____ arms. It can _____
   things in its hands.

2 **Look at the words on the left.** Cross out the phrase on the right which *doesn't* make sense.

1. control	the temperature	~~the instructions~~	the car
2. design	a sea	a building	a robot
3. follow	the rules	the instructions	the keyboard
4. send	a letter	an email	a mouse
5. help	a chore	someone	your mum
6. improve	the conditions	the design	the doctor
7. bring	a coat	a mistake	a towel
8. hold	hands	a hospital	the door

3 **Listen.** David is a robotics engineer. Circle the correct word. 🎧 023

1. I **hold** / **help** to build robots.

2. I **send** / **design** the plans.

3. We decide which parts will be **move** / **movable**.

4. We **follow** / **improve** the plans.

5. We **control** / **follow** this with 'prototype testing'.

6. We **hold** / **control** how we make the robot better.

4 **Listen again.** Number the sentences in the sequence you hear them. 🎧 024

1. He designs the plans needed to build a robot. ☐

2. He works with a lot of other people. ☐

3. He does 'prototype testing'. ☐

4. He goes back and improves plans. ☐

5. David helps to build robots. 1

6 They decide which parts will be movable. ☐

5 **Design and draw a robot.** Then write a description. Use words from the box.

| bring | control | follow | help | hold | improve |

GRAMMAR

Can and *can't*: Talking about ability

I **can** walk.

You **can** sing.

He **can** read.

We **can't** understand the instructions.

They **can't** design new equipment.

Questions

Can you pass me the book, please?

Can it run? Yes, it can.

You use *can* to say what you're able to do:
I **can** *speak three languages.* = *I'***m able to speak** *three languages.*

You don't use *to* with *can*: *I can ~~to~~ speak three languages. Can* and
can't don't change form: ***I can*** *control the robot and* **he can** *control it, too.*

To form the negative, add *'t*: *They* **can't** *get the robot to walk.* = *They* **aren't able to** *get the robot to walk.*

To ask a question, change the word order: ***Can you*** *help me?* ***Can it*** *speak?* ***Can't it*** *fly?*

1 **Rewrite these sentences using *can* or *can't*.**

1. The robot isn't able to communicate with other robots.

   The robot can't communicate with other robots.

2. Today, doctors are able to use robots for operations.

   _____

3. Engineers are able to design movable body parts.

   _____

4. These robots aren't able to understand voice instructions.

   _____

5. This robot isn't able to do chores.

   _____

6. Scientists are able to use robots for exploration.

   _____

2 **Listen to the descriptions.** Number the pictures. 🎧025

3 **Listen again.** Complete the sentences using *can* or *can't*. 🎧026

1. Tobor _____ *can* _____ see what's behind it.

2. Tobor _____ understand the boy's voice.

3. The girl's brother _____ play tennis very well.

4. The girl _____ always hit the ball back to Ballboy.

5. Elgar _____ sing and play the piano.

6. Elgar and the boy _____ improve a song together.

7. The girl _____ remember her dreams.

8. Sylvie _____ tell the girl her dreams.

4 **Answer the questions.**

1. What can you make? _____

2. What can't you do? _____

3. What can you improve? _____

4. What can't you change? _____

Tug-of-war

A gecko

Tiny Robot, # BIG PLANS

Tiny robots can carry 2,000 times their own weight!

¹ Question: What have tug-of-war and geckos got in common? Answer: 'sticky' feet! In tug-of-war, you use your arms, but you also push your feet into the ground. And geckos can walk up most things – even across ceilings. Put the two together, add some engineering, and meet MicroTug.

² MicroTug is small but strong. A 9 g (0.3 oz) MicroTug can pull a 1 kg (2 lb) object up a glass wall. The engineers say this is similar to a person climbing a tall building ... while carrying an elephant!

³ So, how do you design a robot to carry such heavy weights? First, think about how ants can carry big leaves. Then, look at how geckos can walk up walls. They can do this because of the tiny 'hairs' on their feet.

⁴ The design of the robot is simple, but underneath it's got tiny, 'sticky' feet. Scientists use code to program the robot. Then, when MicroTug pulls something heavy, it 'sticks' its feet to the ground and uses a movable part to pull the object.

⁵ Scientists want MicroTug to help people. It might deliver equipment to people trapped in buildings. Or, it might just bring you a drink while you're studying!

42

2 **Match each paragraph with a description.** Write the number.

1. _____ Suggestions about the ways MicroTug might be used in the future.

2. _____ An explanation of what MicroTug can do.

3. _____ An explanation of how MicroTug works.

4. _____ An explanation of where the idea behind MicroTug came from.

5. _1_ An introduction to the topic.

3 **Complete the paragraph with words from the box.**

code	design	engineering	movable	program	project

Put 'sticky' feet and (1) _____ together, and meet MicroTug. The tiny robot can

carry very heavy weights by using its 'sticky' feet and a (2) _____ part. Scientists

use (3) _____ to (4) _____ the robot. The scientists on the

MicroTug (5) _____ want the robot to help people: it might help people trapped

in a building, or it might just bring you something to drink!

4 **Imagine you are on the MicroTug team.** Write a sentence for each stage of the development.
Use words from the box.

code	design	engineer	help	improve	program	project	study

MicroTug	Research	Study how ants can carry things and how geckos can 'stick' to things.
	Design	
	Development	
	Testing	
	Use	

GRAMMAR

Should and *shouldn't*: Giving advice

I **should** read more books in English.
You **should** take your phone with you.
She **should** follow the instructions.
We **shouldn't** bring our pet robots to school.
You **shouldn't** post mean things online.

Questions

Should I learn how to code?
Should they apply to do a computer science course?

You use *should* to talk about the right thing to do: I **should** do my homework as soon as I get home.

You don't use *to* with *should*: We should ~~to~~ find the exit now. Should and shouldn't don't change form: **I should** do my homework. and **She should** read a book.

To form the negative, add *n't* to *should*: We **shouldn't** stay up too late.

To ask a question, change the word order: **Should** we cross the bridge?

1 **Match the sentences.** Write the letter on the line.

_____ 1. I want to learn how to code.

_____ 2. Mary is so tired every day.

_____ 3. They can't go in the water because it's too deep.

_____ 4. I want to get rid of this pain in my leg.

_____ 5. My phone sometimes rings in the cinema.

_____ 6. I want to send this email.

a. She shouldn't go to bed so late.

b. You should see a doctor.

c. You should click this icon, here.

d. You should join a coding club.

e. They should send a robot there instead.

f. You should turn your phone off.

2 **Listen.** Write *should* or *shouldn't*. 🎧 **028**

1. Jasmine _____ study maths.

2. She _____ study design and technology.

3. She _____ listen to her brother's advice.

4. She _____ give up doing art.

5. She _____ continue with a creative subject.

6. She _____ do some online research.

3 **Read Anna's blog.** Use the ideas in the article or your own ideas to write six pieces of advice using *should* and *shouldn't*.

Jobs for the girls!

Right, boys! Get ready for the girls!

It's true that at the moment, more men than women have STEM (science, technology, engineering and maths) jobs. But don't think that this will always be true. If teachers in schools get girls interested in studying maths and computer-based subjects, there's no reason why girls shouldn't play a big part in this type of work. So, what should you girls do? First, don't think that this should be work just for men. Study hard, learn how to code, join a club, play a lot of computer games, watch science fiction films and do online research. If you want to build a robot that changes the world, you should believe that you can! Remember, girls, these jobs aren't just for the boys!

Boys	Girls	Teachers
Boys should get ready for the girls.		

4 **Choose one of the situations.** Write a list of advice for your friend. Use *should* and *shouldn't*.

1. Your friend wants to start up a coding club.

2. Your friend spends six hours every night playing computer games.

3. Your friend isn't very good at maths, but she wants to become an engineer.

4. Your friend loves making robots but doesn't think she should do this as a job.

_____

_____

_____

WRITING

Use words like *but* and *however* when you want to contrast, or show the difference between, two things.

We usually use *but* to join two pieces of contrasting information to make one sentence.
*I should learn to code, **but** there's no coding club at school.*

We usually use *however* at the beginning of a sentence.
*The robots are the same size. **However**, they do very different things.*

1 **Organise.**

1. Compare two different gadgets in your house. Before you start, walk around your house and write down a list of gadgets that you can see. Decide which two gadgets you want to compare. Think about what each gadget is like and what you can and can't do with it. Make notes in the table.

	Smartphone	Computer
Size		
Features		
What you can do with it	play games, make phone calls	do homework
What you can't do with it		

2. Plan your writing. Look at the information about each gadget and write a topic sentence.

   Topic sentence:

   _____ and _____ are both gadgets in my home. They're

   both _____ , but they are very different.

3. Now, use the information to plan your paragraphs. Think about each gadget's size and features. Think about what each gadget can and can't do. Include information on how useful each gadget is. Remember to use contrasing words such as *but* and *however*.

2 **Write.**

1. Go to page 73 in your Student's Book. Re-read the model text.
2. Write your first draft. Check for organisation, content, punctuation, capitalisation and spelling.
3. Write your final draft. Share it with your teacher and classmates.

Now I can ...

· **talk about robots, STEM subjects and gadgets.**

☐ Yes, I can!
☐ I think I can.
☐ I need more practice.

Write two sentences about one of the robots in this unit.

_____

_____

Write two sentences about STEM subjects.

_____

_____

· **use *can* and *can't* to talk about ability.**

☐ Yes, I can!
☐ I think I can.
☐ I need more practice.

Write sentences about things you can and can't do.

_____

_____

Imagine you have a robot. Write sentences about your robot.

_____

_____

· **use *should* and *shouldn't* to give advice.**

☐ Yes, I can!
☐ I think I can.
☐ I need more practice.

Write four sentences using these prompts and *should* or *shouldn't*.

girls / study / coding _____

children / play / a lot of computer games _____

passengers / use / mobile phones / aeroplane _____

engineers / study / science _____

· **contrast two things using the words *but* and *however.***

☐ Yes, I can!
☐ I think I can.
☐ I need more practice.

Write two sentences contrasting robots with real animals. Choose either MicroTug and a real gecko, or Paro and a real baby seal. Use *but* and *however*.

_____

_____

YOU DECIDE **Choose an activity.** Go to page 106.

47

Unit 4
Part of Nature

1 **Complete each sentence with a word from the box.** Then match the photos with the sentences. Write the number.

area	captivity	conservation	costumes	endangered	forest	grow	~~wild~~	workers

1. There aren't many red pandas left in the _____wild_____ .   [d]

2. The Amazon rain forest covers a huge _____ of Brazil.   [ ]

3. The scientist is looking for birds in the _____ .   [ ]

4. Water _____ projects are especially important in dry countries.   [ ]

5. Scientists sometimes wear _____ when they work with animals.   [ ]

6. The sanctuary has a team of _____ that washes the elephants.   [ ]

7. Some of the animals are kept in _____ so they can breed.   [ ]

8. Palm trees _____ in hot and humid climates.   [ ]

a.

b.

c.

d.

e.

f.

g.

h.

2 **Listen.** Read and write **T** for *True* or **F** for *False*. Then rewrite the false statements to make them true. 🎧**029**

1. There are now only 20 whooping cranes in the wild. _____

2. Crane chicks are born in captivity every year. _____

3. Today, workers don't wear costumes or use puppets. _____

4. Adult cranes learn to look after the chicks. _____

5. The cranes learn to live with humans. _____

6. The young cranes stay at the centre for five years. _____

_____

_____

_____

3 **Complete the sentences about giant pandas.** Use words from the box.

| big | captivity | endangered | forests | snow leopards | the wild | workers |

1. Giant pandas live in bamboo _____ in China.

2. There are 1,800 in _____ .

3. They live in _____ areas of land.

4. The _____ try to teach the pandas how to live in the wild.

5. The Sichuan Giant Panda sanctuaries also help _____ .

6. Today, the number of giant pandas is growing. This means they aren't

_____ .

4 **Answer the questions.**

1. What do red pandas and snow leopards have in common? _____

2. Where does bamboo grow? _____

3. Where are animals and plants protected? _____

GRAMMAR

Quantifiers: Talking and asking about quantity

How much ...?	**How much** water do plants need?	There are plants that need **a lot of** water.
		Other plants need **little** water.
		Few plants need no water at all.
How many ...?	**How many** types of leopard are there?	**A lot**. About eight or nine I think.

We use quantifiers to talk about the quantity, or number, of something. When asking about quantities, we use *How much* with uncountable nouns, and *How many* with countable nouns.

We can use *a lot of* with countable and uncountable nouns.

We use *few* with countable nouns: *There are **few** poisonous snakes.* = *There **aren't many** poisonous snakes.*

We use *little* with uncountable nouns: *There's **little** interest in the subject.* = *There **isn't much** interest in the subject.*

1 Complete the questions using *How much* or *How many*.

1. _____ honey can these bees make?

2. _____ bees live in the hive?

3. _____ eyes has a bee got?

4. _____ flowers does a bee visit in one day?

5. _____ time does a bee spend on each flower?

6. _____ eggs does a queen bee lay?

2 **Listen.** Write the words you hear. 🎧 030

I'm walking through the rain forest in Puerto Rico. I can hear (1) _____ different sounds, but I can see very (2) _____ animals! Listen! I can hear insects, mammals and (3) _____ birds, way up in the trees. However, I can see very (4) _____ of them. It's dark here. Very (5) _____ sunlight reaches the forest floor. There are (6) _____ good hiding places for the animals that live here. There's (7) _____ chance of staying dry – everything is soaking wet. There's (8) _____ rain in the forest! Look! What's that? I think it's a snake. I don't know exactly (9) _____ snakes there are in the wild here, but I think there are very (10) _____ .

3 **Look at the photos.** Read and label the fact cards. Then use the information on each card to answer the questions.

elephant   giraffe   jaguar

Animal: _____

Height: 60–80 centimetres
Tail length: 80 centimetres
Weight: 100–160 kilograms
Diet: fish, mammals, reptiles

Animal: _____

Height: 3–4 metres
Tail length: 1–1.5 metres
Weight: up to 8,000 kilograms
Diet: grass, plants
Water per day: 190 litres

Animal: _____

Height: 4–6 metres
Tail length: 1 metre
Weight: 790–1,200 kilograms
Diet: leaves
Water per day: 45 litres

1. How tall is a giraffe? _____

2. How much water does a giraffe drink? _____

3. How much does a jaguar weigh? _____

4. How long is a giraffe's tail? _____

5. How much water does an elephant drink? _____

6. How tall is an elephant? _____

7. How long is a jaguar's tail? _____

8. How much does an elephant weigh? _____

4 **Choose an animal.** Research some facts and write your own fact card. Then ask and answer questions with a partner. Think about the questions below.

How tall is the animal?

How long is the animal's tail?

How much does the animal weigh?

What does the animal eat?

How much water does the animal drink?

Animal: _____
_____
_____
_____
_____
_____

Saving Ghana's Giant Squeaker Frogs

Gilbert Baase Adum holding an African tiger frog

Gilbert Baase Adum doesn't hunt frogs anymore. In fact, he helps save them. Today, he's a leading conservationist and an expert on African frogs. Some frogs are endangered in Ghana, and a lot of people thought the giant squeaker frog was extinct. But thanks to Gilbert's work, these frogs have a second chance.

The land where the frogs live provides the local community with food, fuel and water. However, some people cut down the trees, which is against the law, to use the land for farming. Some local people even burn down the trees to look for bees. The bees make wild honey. When people find the honey, they sell it at local markets.

In 2009, Gilbert found a small population of giant squeaker frogs. Now, he works with his organisation, *Save the Frogs Ghana!*, to protect them. He talks to local farmers and persuades them to find different ways to earn money. He plants trees so that the frogs can return to the area again. He encourages the local community to look after the frogs. He visits schools to tell children how important the frogs are to the community.

Giant squeaker frog

Gilbert knows how important the frogs are. They eat mosquitoes that spread malaria. Malaria is a disease that kills hundreds of thousands of people, including many children, every year. So, Gilbert says that if we save the frogs, we save the world.

2 **Read *Saving Ghana's Giant Squeaker Frogs* again.** Complete the flow chart with the sentences in the box to show the correct sequence of events.

> Gilbert finds giant squeaker frogs.
> Gilbert teaches people about giant squeaker frogs.
> Gilbert is now an expert on African frogs.
> Gilbert helps save giant squeaker frogs.
> Gilbert creates an organisation to protect giant squeaker frogs.

1 People think giant squeaker frogs are extinct.

2

3

4

5

3 **Complete the sentences.**

1. Cutting down trees to use the land for farming is _____.

2. Some people want to find honey _____.

3. Gilbert plants trees so that the frogs can _____.

4. Saving the frogs means saving _____.

GRAMMAR

Adverbs of manner: Saying how you do something

Adjective	Adverb
The giant squeaker frog has got a **loud** squeak.	The giant squeaker frog squeaks **loudly**.
Mountain goats are **good** climbers.	Mountain goats can climb **well**.
It is **easy** for leopards to find prey.	Leopards can find prey **easily**.

We use adverbs of manner to say how we do something. We usually add -ly to an adjective:
*He talks quiet**ly**. She sings happi**ly**.*

When an adjective ends in y (*happy, angry*), we change the y to *i* before adding -ly:
*The lion roared angr**ily**.*

Some words don't change their form: *The cheetah ran **fast**. They worked very **hard**.*

1 **Look at these adjectives.** Write the adverb.

1. happy _____happily_____

2. good _____

3. bad _____

4. quick _____

5. safe _____

6. easy _____

7. fast _____

8. beautiful _____

9. healthy _____

10. slow _____

2 **Read the sentences on the left.** Then complete the sentences on the right with the adverb.

1. Most dogs are good at swimming.　　Most dogs can swim ___well___.

2. Snakes are very quiet when they move.　　Snakes move very _____.

3. Nature photographers are very patient.　　Nature photographers wait _____.

4. Cheetahs are fast runners.　　Cheetahs can run very _____.

5. Sam's homework is always neat.　　Sam always does his homework _____.

6. Joe thinks it's easy to speak English.　　Joe speaks English _____.

7. An elephant's call is very loud.　　Elephants call very _____.

8. Honey bees are hard working.　　Honey bees work very _____.

3 **Read the letter from Leon's grandma.** Circle the correct words. Then listen and check.
🎧 032

> Dear Leon,
>
> I hope you're (1) **happy** / **happily** at your new school. Here's some
> (2) **helpful** / **helpfully** advice for you.
> • Make sure you eat (3) **healthy** / **healthily**.
> • Do your homework (4) **neat** / **neatly**. (5) **Good** / **Well** handwriting
>   is important.
> • Speak (6) **clear** / **clearly** when you talk to your teachers.
> • Learn your spelling every week! It's important to be able to spell
>   (7) **correct** / **correctly**.
> • Be (8) **polite** / **politely**. Don't behave (9) **bad** / **badly**.
> • Be (10) **kind** / **kindly** to people.
> • Play football (11) **good** / **well** and make sure you run (12) **fast** / **fastly**!
> I hope it works out (13) **perfect** / **perfectly** for you.
>
> Lots of love,
> Grandma

4 **Do word sums.** Write **T** for *True* or **F** for *False*.

	A	B	C
1	Cats	swim	well
2	Giraffes	jump	fast
3	Parrots	fly	easily
4	Lions	shout	quietly
5	Frogs	roar	loudly

1. A1 + B3 + C1 = ___Cats fly well._____ [F]

2. A2 + B4 + C5 = _____ [ ]

3. A5 + B2 + C3 = _____ [ ]

4. A4 + B5 + C4 = _____ [ ]

5 **Now make two true sentences about the animals in the table or any others you know.**

1. _____

2. _____

WRITING

When we write a fact sheet, it's important to make sure we check all the facts carefully.

We want the information in a fact sheet to be clearly presented to the reader so that it's easy for them to read. Separate the facts into different sections. Use sub-headings or bullet points to do this.

1 **Organise.**

1. Write a fact sheet about an animal. You can choose an animal from your Student's Book, or any other animal. First, decide which animal you want to write about. Write its name on the line below.

_____

Now look at the list of sub-headings below. Use the library or Internet to find out facts about your animal. Write your facts in the table below.

Colour	
Size (height / weight / length)	
Diet	
Habitat	
Fun facts	

2. Plan your writing. Look at the information in the table above. Think about how to organise your facts. Remember, if you have more than one fact under a heading, you can use bullet points. You also need to include a good introductory sentence. This might include some of your general facts, e.g. *The ... is a large, hairy mammal.* Look at the information above and write your own introductory sentence.

_____

2 **Write.**

1. Go to page 89 in your Student's Book. Re-read the model text.
2. Write your first draft. Check for organisation, content, punctuation, capitalisation and spelling.
3. Write your final draft. Share it with your teacher and classmates.

Now I can ...

· talk about different things in nature.

☐ Yes, I can!
☐ I think I can.
☐ I need more practice.

Use words from the box to write two sentences.

| captivity | conservation | giant panda | giant squeaker frog |

1. _____

2. _____

· use quantifiers to talk about quantity.

☐ Yes, I can!
☐ I think I can.
☐ I need more practice.

Complete these questions and answers. Use *How much / How many* in the questions, and *a lot, little* and *few* in the answers.

1. _____ rain is there in the desert? There's _____ rain in the desert.

2. _____ water can a camel drink in 13 minutes? _____ !

3. _____ wild Bactrian camels are there? _____ .

· use adverbs of manner.

☐ Yes, I can!
☐ I think I can.
☐ I need more practice.

Write three sentences using these words.

| badly | fast | safely |

_____

_____

_____

· write a fact sheet.

☐ Yes, I can!
☐ I think I can.
☐ I need more practice.

Complete the mini fact sheet. Check the details in your Student's Book.

Giant Pandas

Giant pandas live in bamboo _____ in China.

Appearance: • Giant pandas have got _____ and _____ fur.

Diet: • Giant pandas' favourite food is _____ .

Population: • There are _____ giant pandas in the wild.

Units 3–4 Review

1 **Read.** Choose the word that best completes the sentences.

1. There are few rhinoceros in the wild. They are an ____ species.
   a. endangered   b. against the law   c. engineering

2. Some pandas live in ____, where workers can look after them.
   a. the wild   b. costumes   c. captivity

3. Robotic cameras are used in ____ projects. They can see animals in certain areas.
   a. boring   b. conservation   c. control

4. Robots are also used in hospitals, to ____ people with pain.
   a. code   b. grow   c. help

5. The engineer is designing a robotic hand with ____ fingers.
   a. online
   b. movable
   c. wild

6. The baby leopard only weighs two ____.
   a. litres
   b. centimetres
   c. kilograms

2 **Listen.** Circle the correct response for each sentence you hear. 🎧 033

1. a. No, the workers should return the robot.
   b. Yes, but I dream about robots cleaning my house.

2. a. It's a conservation project.
   b. Yes, they can return to this area.

3. a. No, they shouldn't cry.
   b. Yes, they can code very well.

4. a. That's fantastic!
   b. That's against the law.

3 **Read the blog post.** Decide which answer (**a**, **b** or **c**) best fits each gap.

Becoming a Great Photographer

I love taking photographs. I take photos of birds, plants, animals and insects. Sometimes, I wait (1) ____ for hours, just to see a bee land on a flower. Getting a great photo takes (2) ____ of patience.

Do you want to be a photographer? Think about these ideas as you get started:

- You (3) ____ think carefully about what you want to photograph.

- You (4) ____ get great photos with the right location. Think about it: (5) ____ different plants or birds can you photograph in one place? You don't want to choose a place with (6) ____ interesting things to photograph.

- Think about (7) ____ time you can spend taking photos.

- How good is your camera? A poor camera can (8) ____ make a photo come out (9) ____.

- You (10) ____ expect your first shot to be perfect!

1.	a. loudly	b. well	c. quietly	**6.**	a. a lot	b. little	c. few
2.	a. few	b. a lot	c. little	**7.**	a. how much	b. how many	c. how easily
3.	a. should	b. shouldn't	c. can't	**8.**	a. high	b. easily	c. well
4.	a. shouldn't	b. can't	c. can	**9.**	a. badly	b. good	c. little
5.	a. how much	b. how many	c. how well	**10.**	a. can	b. should	c. shouldn't

4 **Match the questions with the answers.** Write the letter on the line.

____ 1. How much time do you spend taking photos?

____ 2. Can you easily photograph the bees?

____ 3. Should you be very loud at work?

____ 4. Can robots take better photos than people?

____ 5. How does she work?

____ 6. Should you tell someone where you're going?

____ 7. How many cameras have you got?

____ 8. How many bees are in this area?

a. No, you can't.

b. No, they can't.

c. Two.

d. A lot!

e. There are very few.

f. Yes, you should.

g. No, you shouldn't.

h. She works quietly.

☐ **1** Use words from the box to talk about people in your family.

child	daughter	friendly
good at	husband	is married to
son	wife	

☐ **2** Use *be* and *have got*, plus words from the box, to describe yourself.

annoying	aunt/uncle	brother/sister
funny	interested in	mean
mother/father	noisy	

_____

_____

_____

_____

☐ **3** Use *some* or *any* to say if the following items are or aren't in your fridge.

apples	biscuits	bread	cheese
juice	milk	toys	yoghurt

☐ **4** **Work in pairs.** Research a popular dish from another country. Choose a different country to your partner. Tell your partner about your dish. Include:

- where it's from
- its ingredients
- how it's made
- when people eat it
- why it's popular
- if you want to try it

☐ **5** **Write.** Describe a close friend. Use *and* and *but* in your description.

- To plan your writing, follow the steps on page 24 of your Workbook.
- Share your writing with your teacher and classmates.

☐ **6** **Write.** You see this poster in your school.

Bring a Family Member to School Day!

Students! Choose a family member to bring to school on Friday, 3rd March.

This person can learn about your school day and meet your friends and teachers.

Which family member do you choose? Why do you want this person to visit your school? Write 50–80 words.

1 Use words from the box to talk about school.

classmate	difficult	easy
homework	lesson	library
(once/twice) a week	practise	

2 Use the present simple of verbs from the box to say what you do and don't do.

do	eat	get up	go
make	practise	take	walk

3 Complete each sentence with true information. Use an adverb of frequency.

1. I _____ use the Internet.

2. Our teacher _____ gives us homework at the weekend.

3. I _____ play tennis.

4. My family _____ eats breakfast together.

5. I _____ go to the library.

4 **Work in pairs.** Role-play an interview about school life between a current student and a new student. Include details on:

- the timetable
- the lessons
- after-school activities/clubs
- the teachers
- what's special about your school

5 **Write.** Imagine you're a teacher at your school. Write an article for a school magazine about your daily routine. Remember to use words such as *first*, *next*, *then*, *before* and *after*.

- To plan your writing, follow the steps on page 34 of your Workbook.
- Share your writing with your teacher and classmates.

6 **Write.** You see this advertisement in your school newspaper.

After-school Clubs

Next term, we want to start new after-school clubs. What new clubs do you want? How many times a week do you want them? Please give us your ideas.

Reply to the advertisement. Write your suggestion for an after-school club. Say why it's a good idea and how often you want to do it. Write 50–80 words.

1 Talk about robots. Use words from the box.

bring	code	control	design
follow	help	hold	improve
movable	program		

2 Talk about what robots *can* and *can't* do. Use words from the box.

cry	dream	hold	imagine
laugh	love	move	think

3 Say whether you think robots *should* or *shouldn't* do each activity for you.

1. do homework
2. tidy up
3. cook dinner
4. teach languages
5. mend (a bicycle, a car, etc.)
6. go shopping

4 **Work in pairs.** Think about what job you want to do. Use words from the box or your own ideas. Tell your partner about your job. Then listen as he or she gives advice on how to prepare for it. Your partner will tell you two things you should do, and one thing you shouldn't do. When you finish, swap roles.

climber	designer	engineer
explorer	footballer	musician
photographer	roboticist	teacher
scientist		

Example: *To be a musician, you should learn to read music. You should practise every day. You shouldn't miss practice.*

5 **Write.** Choose a real or imaginary robot. Compare it to a human. Use *but* and *however* to talk about what it can and can't do.

- To plan your writing, follow the steps on page 46 of your Workbook.
- Draw a picture of your robot.
- Share your writing and picture with your teacher and classmates.

6 **Write.** Imagine a story with the following title:

My best friend is a robot.

Write your story. Write 60–100 words.

YOU DECIDE Choose an activity. Unit 4

1 Choose one of the animals from the first box. Then use words from the second box to talk about it.

| camel | capybara | leopard | panda |

captivity	conservation	endanger
forest	kilogram	metre
mountain	reserve	

2 Ask questions using *How much* and *How many* and the words below. Then use the information in your Student's Book to answer the questions.

- pandas / be / in the wild
- capybara / weigh
- water / Bactrian camel / drink
- Bactrian camels / be / in the wild
- animals / poachers / take from the rainforest

Example: *How many pandas are there in the wild? There are 1,800 pandas in the wild.*

3 Read the sentences. Then complete them with an adverb.

1. Dolphins are good swimmers. They swim very _____.

2. Cheetahs are fast runners. They run _____.

3. Sloths are slow animals. They move very _____.

4. The mother lion is careful with her babies. She carries them _____ in her mouth.

5. The monkeys climb to the top of the trees. They climb up very _____.

4 Work in pairs. Role-play an interview with a conservationist.

- Research people who work on conservation projects.
- Choose one conservationist. Prepare three questions to ask about the work he/she does. Make notes about the answers to your questions.
- Assign the roles of interviewer and conservation worker.
- Practise the interview with your partner.
- Act out the interview in class, or record it on a phone or tablet.

5 Write. Use the Internet to learn about reserves or conservation areas around the world. Choose one and write a fact sheet about it. Include information on where it is, what animals and plants are there and what problem it wants to solve.

- To plan your writing, follow the steps on page 56 of your Workbook.
- Share your writing with your teacher and classmates.

6 Write. You need to write a fact sheet about an animal called a caribou. Your friend's father works with caribou in North America. Continue the email to him. Ask him questions for your fact sheet.

From: analee123@anyemail.com

Dear Mr Madry,

I am writing a fact sheet on caribou. I need to find answers to some questions. Please can you help? I want to know …

Finish the email. Write about 100 words.